Twayne's English Authors Series

Sylvia E. Bowman, *Editor*

INDIANA UNIVERSITY

John Evelyn

(TEAS) 144

John Evelyn

By JEANNE K. WELCHER

C. W. Post College

Twayne Publishers, Inc.   : :   New York

Preface

For most readers, John Evelyn is a one-book man. His diary is readily available and well read, but not the rest of his writings. Yet he wrote more than twenty books, a similar number of short formal pieces, and hundreds of letters; he also translated and edited a dozen books by other authors. His works are in the form of essays, biographies, histories, character writings, rules of life, prayers, dedications, debates, satiric prose and poetry, courtesy literature, and polite verse. His topics include gardening, medicine, geography, city planning, air pollution, navigation and commerce, literary criticism, painting and engraving, coins, architecture, libraries, politics, philosophy, and theology. Clearly, Evelyn was the virtuoso par excellence, something of a dilettante perhaps, but with considerable mastery of a staggering variety of subjects and a vibrant interest in them all—indeed, he was one of the very last of the Renaissance gentlemen-encyclopedists.

The works vary greatly in literary pretension and success. Many of them are worth reading for their own sake, and all contribute to a knowledge of the period. Nevertheless, they are relatively little known today, largely because copies of them are scarce. They have never been voluminously printed, and the fifteen which were reprinted in this century are now out of print. Indeed, only very well-stocked libraries include anything besides the diary. Even works about Evelyn as a man of letters are not plentiful. Scholars have studied his life and have analyzed the content of some of his works. Literary analysis of them is, however, scanty. And again, such secondary material as does exist is not readily available.

The aims of this study, consequently, are two. It sets forth the respective merits of Evelyn's writings, so that readers who wish to read them themselves may know which to pursue. Also, it will provide a partial but practical substitute for the works for those readers who cannot get the primary texts or whose interest in Evelyn is as a context for other material.

Chapters 1–4 examine all of Evelyn's published works except his diary and letters. Most of these were written expressly for publication and did appear during Evelyn's lifetime, some signed by him and some under a pseudonym. The posthumous publications are works which Evelyn substantially completed but never himself issued. Manuscript material which has never been printed is occasionally referred to but it is not discussed in detail. Each published work is described and analyzed, in terms of itself, and in terms of its relation to others of its kind. The works are presented in the order of composition. Chapter 5 treats of the correspondence and the diary, works which spanned Evelyn's life. The last chapter provides generalizations about Evelyn's position in English literature and his contributions to literary history.

Because of the rarity of Evelyn's works, this book could never have been written without the very good services of many libraries and reference librarians, notably the Avery Architectural Library of Columbia University, the Cornell University Library, the New York Public Library, the University of Virginia and Virginia State Libraries, the Chapin Library of Williams College, and the Yale University Library. Thanks are also due to associates and friends who made suggestions and read and criticized my manuscript. My special indebtedness is to Eileen Corrigan, to John Kaiser, and to Therese Kreier.

All quotations from Evelyn's diary are taken from the edition made by E. S. de Beer (1955), by permission of the Clarendon Press, Oxford. All quotations from Evelyn's correspondence, unless otherwise noted, are from H. B. Wheatley's four-volume 1906 edition of the *Diary;* in the text, I cite them by date only. Because it is more generally available than the individual editions, *The Miscellaneous Writings* (1825) is used as the source for quotations from the texts which it reprints; after each first reference, these are cited with only a page number.

J. K. WELCHER

C. W. Post College
Brookville, New York

Contents

Chronology

1620   John Evelyn born, at family estate, Wotton, in Surrey.

1630   First notes toward his diary.

1637–   Attendance at Balliol College, Oxford.
1640

1641   Trip through the Netherlands.

1641–   Residence in London and Wotton.
1643

1643–   Travels through France and Italy.
1647

1647   Marriage in Paris to Mary Browne.

1647–   Return to England and residence there.
1649

1649   Publication of his first book, the translation *Of Liberty and Servitude.*

1649–   Return to England, settling at the Browne family estate,
1652   Sayes Court, in Deptford; publication of his first original work, *The State of France;* birth of first child, Richard.

1654   Tour of England with Mrs. Evelyn.

1655   Birth of John, Jr., the one son to live to adulthood.

1658   Publication of his first book on gardening, the translation *The French Gardiner,* and first reference to *Elysium Britannicum;* death of son Richard; translation and publication of *The Golden Book of St. John Chrysostom, concerning the Education of Children.*

1659   Attempt by Evelyn to enlist Colonel Morley to aid in Restoration.

1659–   Publication of pamphlets in connection with Restoration.
1661

1661   Membership in Royal Society and Evelyn's first paper; publication of *Fumifugium* and *Tyrannus.*

1662 Appointment as a commissioner for London streets; first mention of the history of trades; publication of *Sculptura*.

1663 Appointment as a commissioner of the Mint.

1664 Publication of *Sylva*.

1664– Active as a commissioner for sick and wounded seamen,
1667 in connection with Second Dutch War.

1665– Plague in London.
1666

1666 Great Fire of London; presentation of *Londinium Redivivum*.

1667 Publication of *Publick Employment and an Active Life Prefer'd to Solitude;* gift of Arundelian Marbles to Oxford, at Evelyn's instigation.

1669 Publication of *The History of Three Late Famous Impostors;* award to Evelyn of honorary degree by Oxford, for his part in gift of Arundelian Marbles; first mention in diary of Samuel Pepys and Margaret Godolphin.

1669– Work on the history of the Dutch War.
1674

1670 Second edition of *Sylva*.

1671– Appointment to Council for Foreign Plantations.
1674

1672– Active, as a commissioner for sick and wounded seamen,
1674 in connection with Second Dutch War.

1672 Pact of friendship between Evelyn and Margaret Godolphin.

1674 Publication of *Navigation and Commerce*.

1678 Death of Mrs. Godolphin.

1678– Composition of *A Devotionarie Book,* left in mss.
1685

1679 Third edition of *Sylva*.

1681 Negotiator representing Royal Society in sale of Chelsea College for use as military hospital.

1682 Birth of Evelyn's first grandson, John (later Sir John Evelyn).

1682– Probable period of composition of *The Life of Mrs. Godol-*
1684 *phin,* left in mss.

1683 Commendatory poem to Thomas Creech for his translation of Lucretius.

1685 Death of Evelyn's daughter Mary; elopement and death of his daughter Elizabeth.

1685– Appointment as a commissioner for the Privy Seal.
1687

1686 Probable period of composition of *Directions for the Gardiner at Says-Court,* left in mss.

1688 Probable period of composition of *History of Religion,* left in mss.

1690 Publication by Evelyn of his daughter Mary's *Mundus Muliebris.*

1691 Heir to Wotton.

1692 Appointment as a trustee for the Boyle Lectures.

1693 Marriage of his only surviving daughter, Susanna.

1694 Move from Sayes Court to Wotton; intermittent residence in London.

1695– Appointment as treasurer for Greenwich Hospital.
1703

1697 Publication of *Numismata.*

1698 Peter the Great, tsar of Russia, subtenant of Sayes Court.

1698– Family dispute over succession of Wotton.
1699

1699 Death of John, Jr., Evelyn's last surviving son; succession to Wotton, on death of Evelyn's elder brother, George; publication of *Acetaria.*

1700 Move to Wotton as owner; presentation of plans for Greenwich Hospital made to king by Sir Christopher Wren and Evelyn.

1704 Composition of *Memoires for my Grand-son,* left in mss.

1706 Death of Evelyn; fourth edition of *Silva.*

1818 First publication of Evelyn's diary.

CHAPTER 1

1649-1660—Modest Beginnings
of a Literary Career

JOHN Evelyn has secured a modest but well-recognized place in English literature, as one of the earliest and most comprehensive diarists. In addition to acting as spectator and recorder for his own life and age, he contributed immediately to the contemporary literary scene by publishing some fifty pieces, ranging from brief prefatory verses to voluminous books. The same circumstances in his life which fitted him as diarist-chronicler also provided him with the substance and impetus for this varied writing career.

His eighty-six-year life (1620–1706) covered the reigns of five monarchs and the Commonwealth. He came from landed gentry in Surrey; his father was "a studious decliner of Honors and Titles," as was John in his turn (Diary, Oct. 31, 1620). The family background provided him with an introduction to the first families, including royalty. He was given intellectual and cultural training and such education as he wished—although, in his three years at Balliol College, Oxford, he took part in the college life only about half the time because of ill-health and family affairs, "so as my being at the University, in reguard of these avocations, was of very small benefit to me" (Diary, Apr. 27, 1640). He was free to travel as he wished, and he was assured of financial security throughout his life.

His travels started in the Low Countries where he combined sightseeing with a taste of military life. He quickly rejected the latter, "for the sun peircing the Canvass of the Tent, it was during the day unsufferable, and at night, not seldome infested by the mists and foggs, which ascended from the river . . . so that being prety well satisfied with the confusion of Armies, & seiges . . . I tooke my leave" (Diary, Aug. 3–8, 1641). Traveling suited him better. Intermittently for some ten years he familiarized himself with the art, culture, and customs of the Continent. He learned the languages and attended courses, particularly in the sciences. He purchased books, curiosities, and antiquities; paid his court to the English royalty in exile; and married Mary Browne, the daughter of the English Resident with the French Court. In spite of the civil war in England, Evelyn made short visits there; and, remarkably, he was able to maintain sufficient peace with the Commonwealth government that neither his property nor his freedom was curtailed.

In 1652 he and his wife settled on her father's estate, Sayes Court, which was near enough London for frequent trips but far enough that there were grounds adequate for terraces, promenades, greens, groves, and gardens of every sort. For forty years at Sayes Court, before becoming heir to his own family estate of Wotton in Surrey, Evelyn reared his children, worshiped, entertained, and developed his garden, library, and museum. He served on the London Streets Commission, the Mint Committee, and the Council for Foreign Plantations. He held the offices of commissioner for sick and wounded seamen and commissioner for the Privy Seal. Of far more importance in his own eyes than these civic posts, he was a Fellow of the Royal Society from its inception in 1661 onward.

All the while, he wrote at an amazing rate, producing an abundance of material on many different subjects in a great variety of forms. The diary, begun at an early age, was his first exercise. In 1649 he started to write for publication, and he did not stop until shortly before his death. In these years he published eighteen original books and pamphlets, a dozen translations and editions, and about twenty shorter pieces such as articles for journals and other edited volumes as well as commendatory verse and introductions. He left completed, in manuscript, several books, essays, and elaborate outlines that have been posthumously published, as well as copious letters, notebooks, and other manuscripts that have not yet been issued to the public.

Looking over this body of work in search of groupings, one becomes aware that the pattern is not one of different subjects, genres, or reasons for writing at different periods of his life but a steady, continuous interweaving of Evelyn's many interests. Few subjects that appealed to him early in his writing career palled on him later; no utterly new interests appear later. Within the first ten years of his writing, he touched on all the topics that were to recur: gardening, food, science, the arts, politics, and religion. Both poetry and prose are represented. Some of the works are unadorned exposition; others are genuinely creative.

I *Products of France*

The modest beginning of this prolific writing career is given terse mention in the diary. The time is the ill-fated month of January, 1649; for on the thirtieth of that month, as he tragically records, the villainy of the rebels reached its climax with the execution of Charles I. In his dark and threatening time, Evelyn made bold to issue his first work: "was published my Translation of *Liberty & Servitude*, for the Preface of which I was severly threatn'd" (Diary, Jan. 21, 1649).

De la Liberté et de la Servitude, by F. de La Mothe le Vayer, was published in France in 1643. This essay is a philosophical but not profound examination of the liberty which all wish and the servitude which all have. The culmination of the work is not so much the political or civil scene as court life, which is pessimistically presented: "Courtiers may . . . passe for the most unhappy amongst men" (*Misc. Writ.*, 29). When one considers the inexperience in court life of both La Mothe le Vayer and Evelyn, together with Evelyn's bold preface praising the "excellent form of government . . . under wch we ourselves have lived, during the reign of our most gratious Soveraignes Halcion daies" (6), the denunciation of courtly servitude has a curious flavor in which unintentional irony and untried idealism blend.

The anomaly of simultaneously flattering and condemning the court is the less apparent because of the style of the essay. Evelyn follows La Mothe le Vayer closely but not literally, and the resulting translation, like the original, is detached, mildly skeptical, and always temperate. The firm emphasis on the exaltation of reason gives a constructive quality, but the outlook of the work is scarcely cheerful. By introducing inversions, expanded constructions, and emphasis by means of repetition or additional adverbs, he gives the essay a distinctly seventeenth-century English flavor, one which is genteel rather than polemical, as is indicated by this example from the climax of Chapter I:

And hence it is that the Devil is named in holy-writ Belial, as we should say, one that desired to shake off the yoake, and depend no more upon any. Now since we thus naturally seeke to be free, and so by consequence fly servitude, not onely like the rest of animalls, but much more in respect of that whereby we are distinguished from them; and for that which we communicate with the superior Intelligencies, it implies that men ought to be most free of all sublunary creatures. And yet, notwithstanding all this, it is possible that there is generally, and in all respects, no greater slave than man himselfe. (10) [1]

The phrasing and vocabulary create an air of regret rather than revolt—and of utter reasonableness.

A preface to *Liberty and Servitude* indicates that Evelyn actually did the translation in Paris in 1647, a time when things in England, while bad, were not catastrophic. At that safe distance, to hope that La Mothe le Vayer's good sense might mold some English minds probably did not seem far-fetched. In the words addressed "To him that reades," Evelyn insists that the idea of liberty he has presented is of a practical order, "not that Platonique chimaera of a state, no where existant save in UTOPIA" (5). That he persevered and published the work, when he was in England himself and when all reasonableness seemed to have deserted that country, does smack a bit of utopianism.

The work is technically anonymous, for Evelyn's name does not appear on the title page, and he uses a fanciful pseudonym—Phileleutheros, Lover of Liberty—as the signature for the Translator's Epistle. But that epistle is dedicated familiarly to his brother George, and prefatory Latin verses complimenting the translator address Evelyn by name. Evelyn was not dodging responsibility for the work, but the diary passage quoted above and a marginal note in his own copy of *Liberty & Servitude* indicate that there were threats against him because of the work. In what fashion or by whom he was threatened is not known. Evelyn was as yet far from being a prominent person, but these were perilous times for speaking out.

For the student of Evelyn, the most interesting part of the work is the Translator's Epistle (5) in which Evelyn's tone is almost lighthearted. His abiding pleasure in recondite vocabulary is evident when he tells his brother, not that he is dedicating the work to him, but rather that "I thought most proper to *nuncupate* it

[14]

unto you." His self-consciousness as a beginning author is expressed in an elaborate figure: "This is the first time (as you well know) of mine appearing upon the theater, which I shall prove to frequent but as gentlemen who sometimes write plaies, not often." The picture of Evelyn appearing upon the theater is unlikely enough, without the surprising gulf between the frivolity of this metaphor and the nature of the work itself.

Another early work by Evelyn that likewise took its origins in his European experiences is a little essay called "The Genuine Receipt for Orvietario," the ideas of which came to Evelyn from a French chemist in 1652. During the winter of 1647 Evelyn had lodgings near the medical schools on the Left Bank in Paris; and in February he took a course from Nicasius Le Fèvre, a celebrated medical chemist, later apothecary to Charles II and Fellow of the Royal Society. When the two men became personally acquainted, Le Fèvre gave Evelyn information on how to make orvietan (as it is more commonly spelled), a popular antidote for poison. Evelyn added to the Latin prescription an explanation of the transmission of the receipt; a description of the virtues of this medicine for poisoning, dog bite, fever, pestilence, and cattle disease; and directions for taking it. Just when he wrote this account is not explained; it was posthumously published in an eighteenth-century compilation, *Philosophical Experiments and Observations of the late Eminent Dr. Robert Hooke ... and other Eminent Virtuosos in his Time.*[2]

Evelyn's next book was his first original publication: *The State of France, as it stood in the IXth year of this present Monarch, Lewis XIIII,* published in 1652. It consists of two parts: a lengthy prefatory letter and an essay. In spite of this division, the tone of the entire work is epistolary. The title page carries the signature "Written to a friend by E," and Evelyn tells the friend that he is complying with his request to put in book form the substance of conversations which they had about Evelyn's European travels. He directly addresses the friend throughout both the preface and the essay and ends with a complimentary close.

Whether the friend is real or fictional, one cannot tell. In the convention of the day, Evelyn often protests that he has published a particular work only because someone, venerable or in authority, has insisted. But he usually names his promoter, whereas here he leaves him anonymous; and, once having cited him, he usually makes no further reference to him, but in *The State of France*, the friend plays a definite role. He is characterized as a man more mature than the author, one to whom Evelyn is in some way accountable, apparently not a traveler himself and possibly even a trifle skeptical about the advantages of grand tours. He is an inexhaustible listener, curious for factual details and personal interpretations and challenging in his questions. His attitude has prompted Evelyn to summarize his peregrinations and to think out a justification for travel. The friend's interest seems to be strictly academic, for one finds no indication that he intends to travel himself.

So Evelyn broadens the framework of his account by imagining for his friend the sort of person who conceivably might put these ideas into practice, a young gentleman, ripe for travel, sensitive, relatively immature, and exemplary in his readiness to receive advice. Evelyn, having reconsidered his time abroad, clarifies the proper motivation for travel; sketches an ideal itinerary; and then, brushing aside the friend's demand for an account of each country, chooses one—France—to treat in detail.

The pleasing result of this sketchily conceived triumvirate is that the reader is directly addressed, alternately as a wise old contemplative stay-at-home friend and as an eager young voyager. The principal tone of the work is respectful and deprecatory. The air is not patronizing, despite all the information that is conveyed. Even the potential young traveler is spoken of flatteringly, for the presumption is that he will use his time wisely in all ways, a perfection Evelyn claims not to have achieved.

The first section of the book debates the value of travel. Having presented the usual arguments and cited the authorities, Evelyn somewhat surprisingly rests the defense on the moral results—"surprisingly," because of the frequent English diatribes on the corrupting effects of travel. Also, in his later writings, Evelyn generally stresses science, art, and statesmanship as the areas enriched by travel.[3] But here, he lists these benefits: "truth, taciturnitie, facetiousnesse without morosity, courage, modesty, hardinesse, patience, frugality, and an excellent temper in the regiment of his health and affections, especially in point of drink and tobacco, which is our northerne, nationall, and most sordid of vices . . . it is this ethicall and morall part of travel, which embellisheth a gentleman" (46–47). Likewise he acknowledges the faults of many travelers: shallowness, vanity, triviality, preoccupation with details. He exalts the life of the retired country gentleman. He incorporates an ode which he wrote in Naples, 1645, in which the joys of home and the nuptial bed are proposed as preferable to the madness of the traveler. The cumulative effect is partly wry satire, partly genuine ambivalence.

The main part of *The State of France* presents factual details about the structure of the country: the monarchy, the church, taxes, the parliament, the army, and aristocratic orders. This section, far from exhaustive, describes some fine points and leaves out some large areas. After the facts come generalizations and evaluations about the church and the government, the plebeians and their complaints, the merchants, the aristocracy, religion, soldiers, the state at present, France's foreign relations, learning, and the condition of women and children. The book concludes with the French opinion of the English—"they have a naturall dread and hate to the English, as esteeming us for the most part, a fierce, rude and barbarous nation" (92)—and with a brief description of the beauties of Paris.

The reader who goes to this book for systematic enlightenment on mid-seventeenth-century France will be disappointed. There are plenty of facts, but they are curiously selected and in disarray. There are plenty of judgments, but no attempt is made to distinguish what Evelyn calls "solid opinions" (78) from those uniquely his own. Inferences, predictions, and comparisons (especially with England) abound, largely unsubstantiated and frankly opinionative. The value of the work lies almost wholly outside the informational.

The charm of *The State of France* is in its rhetorical artistry. Evelyn uses persuasively the epistolary, informal essay structure. Not objectively, not logically, but with vitality and volubility, he records one aristocratic Englishman's vision of France during the 1640's. By using homely figures of speech, he implies a speaker who is simple, down-to-earth, utterly honest, and, for these reasons, entirely reliable. Rhetorical devices of parallelism and antithesis suggest the presence of argument by analogy when, in fact, no essential point of comparison has been established. Variety in vocabulary exploits connotative effects. Evelyn does not say that he is the number one Baedeker of his day, but his rhetoric implies as much.

Without being at all specific, Evelyn gives a lively picture of French facial appearance: "The French Children are the fairest letter that Nature, I think, can shew through all the humane alphabet; but though they be Angels in the cradle, yet are they more like Divels in the saddle . . . for the French (after twenty) presently strike forty in their faces" (90). French conviviality is bluntly described: they "have generally their tongues well hung . . . so they are for the most part of joviall conversation, and far from that constrained addresse which is naturall to our sullen nation, who never think ourselves acquainted, till we treat one another with Jack and Tom" (91). The simplicity of the terms makes his approbation or rejection all the more convincing. No matter how in accord one may be with the French taste for soup and fresh bread, Evelyn forces us to see as singular the omnipresence of such fare: they "are strange devourers of corn; they adore a good pottage (whatever the rest of the repast be) as the Egyptians did garlick" (91).

Often the imagery is metaphorical, usually vividly so, and sometimes startling in comparisons. He speaks of affected travelers, those who are untouched by the basic and universal qualities of their neighbors but return imitating their idiosyncrasies, "as one would easily imagine they had all this while lived in pension rather amongst apes and parrots" (45). Compression makes epigrams of many of his observations, as in this description of the superficial traveler: "not every man that crosses the seas, hath been of an academy" (45). Of learning a foreign language, he writes: "it is one of the shels of travel, though I confesse, the kernel is not to be procured without it" (47); the comparison, while fanciful, is persuasive.

How original Evelyn is in these expressions need not be a major concern. When he says the insensitive traveler goes untouched through foreign lands "like a goose swimms down the river," he attributes the expression to "a late Embassador of ours" (46). The most celebrated phrase from *State of France* has been shown to have appeared five years before in a letter to Evelyn, where Thomas Henshaw complained of overdone sightseeing as "counting steeples." [4] Evelyn used the words thus: "It is written of Ulysses, that hee saw many cities indeed, but, with all, his remarks of mens manners and customs was ever preferred to his counting steeples, and making tours" (47). The expression may even have had a currency in these young travelers' circles; but, in writing, it was not hackneyed, and Evelyn uses it tellingly. He clearly had an ear for the precise detail which gave particularity and solidity to his thoughts.

Contrasting with these simple metaphors and somewhat proverbial expressions is his frequent use of hard words. Some are genuinely rare: "apodemick," "Pontificians" (meaning Catholics), "idiopathia," "substruction," "gabels," "pererration," and "elaboratory." Others are only faintly Anglicized: "repatriare," "luxe," "bibliotheke," "in pension." The slightly varied spelling or form distinguishes "mimicall folly," "extravagancies," "imported" (meaning "transported" or "carried away": "women and children . . . are commonly more imported with wonder and romance"), "aboad," "apophtheme," "the perill of disbauched and frequent collationings," "improsperous," and "obnoxious" (meaning "liable" or "subject to"). And some are simply mouth-filling: "perpetuall peregrination," "succinctness and perspicuity," "so prodigious a fatality," "schismatiques and broachers of ridiculous enthusiasms."

In his advice to the young traveler, Evelyn warns against "philologicall peregrinations"—a boastful display of a foreign language which is "onely a parrot-virtue" (47) as opposed to the intelligent application of such an ability. To many a twentieth-century reader, Evelyn's unfamiliar vocabulary and spelling seem very like philological peregrinations and a flavor of quaintness is produced. For Evelyn's contemporaries, however, the effect would have been one of dignity, precision, and just enough erudition to substantiate the writer's authority.

II *Lucretius, Bonnefons, and Chrysostom*

Perhaps while he was preparing *The State of France* for publication, or at least shortly thereafter, Evelyn resumed the work of translation. His next three publications are of this nature, but the likeness ends with the fact of their being translations. For they differ greatly. The languages from which they come are Latin, French, and Greek. The dates of their origin are the first century B.C., the seventeenth century, and the fourth century. The subjects are materialistic philosophy, gardening, and education. One is in verse; the others, in prose.

The first of the three was *An Essay on the first Book of T. Lucretius Carus de Rerum Natura, interpreted and made English verse*, 1656. Evelyn's title for the book is a trifle confusing. The "Essay" so called is, in fact, the text of Book I of the poem; and Latin and English versions appear on facing pages. This material makes up about one third of the volume, Preceding the text are a frontispiece, a preface by Evelyn, and various complimentary letters and verses. After the text come a message from the stationer and a lengthy essay by Evelyn called "Animadversions upon the First Book of T. Lucretius Carus." The frontispiece was designed by Evelyn's wife, Mary, who had some artistic training and who produced for this occasion a pleasant profile view of Lucretius crowned with the usual laurels. The treatment is entirely conventional except in one particular: the model that Mary used for the head, whether consciously or not, was John himself. Considering his eventual ambivalence toward the work, he makes a strange Lucretius the Second.

The preface, "The Interpreter to Him that Reads," is a thoroughly satisfactory little essay in its range of ideas and expression. It deals principally with attitudes toward Lucretius and problems of translating. The need for the first of these is, as Evelyn puts it in his diary, that "little of the Epicurean Philosophy was known then amongst us" (May 12, 1656). The preface anticipates objections from three sorts of people. First are the learned who will protest that Evelyn has "levell'd too great a part of *Philosophy*, such as was locked up for them onely." Evelyn dismisses this group lightly, stressing the values of Lucretius and the likelihood that any who enjoy Book I in translation will then pursue the whole in its original form. Second, the ignorant may "carp at the cadences of the verse . . . such as have little acquaintance with the Original, nor ever so much as once assayed what it was to tamper with Lucretius." To answer these, Evelyn cites Bacon, saying that they may profit from the effort required, for Lucretius is "an excellent *specifique*, and rare ingredient for unstayed and *Bird-witted* men; since that *here*, as *there*, if the minde be not seriously fixed, the *Demonstration* is ever to begin." Third are the scrupulous, whose protests cannot be taken seriously unless one is going to avoid all ancient writers, for "there is none exempt of the most gross and absur'd Fictions, apparent Levities, and horrible Impieties imaginable."

Evelyn was explaining but not apologizing. His self-assurance and ease are reflected in a flowing style and in some particularly handsome rhetorical flourishes. The most elaborate passage compares the texture of Lucretius' verse and thought with the countryside of Lombardy. Students of seventeenth-century taste note the importance of the sensibility he displays here, as Evelyn finds beauty in the intermingling of harsh sublime with placidly pastoral: [5] "where sometimes from the cragginess of inaccessible Rocks, uneven and horrid precipices . . . there breaks and divides (as the Wandring *Traveller* approaches) a passage to his eyes down into some goodly and luxurious valley; where the trembling serpenting of some Chrystal rivolet, frngied with the curtous diaper of the softer meadows, the umbrage & harmonious warbling of the cooler groves . . . recompense him the pain of so many difficult accesses." He applies the simile at some length, finding the same naturalness and variety in Lucretius as in this Italian scene.

Acknowledging indebtedness to Pierre Gassendi, the French critic of Epicurus, for the idea behind another extended comparison, Evelyn concludes his reply to the scrupulous: "No man, I hope, comes hither as a *Spider*, to swell up his bag with *poyson* onely, when with half that pains, he may with the industrious *Bee*, store and furnish his *Hive* with so much wholesome and delicious Honey." Gassendi had expressed the thought by condemning whoever would destroy a rose garden because it contained thorns. Evelyn's image is perhaps not so logically apposite as Gassendi's, but it has the merits of freshness, of association with the many biblical and Classical references to the bee's sweetness and industry, and (for the modern reader) of association with the more celebrated appearances of the same fable in the works of William Temple, Jonathan Swift, and Matthew Arnold.

In presenting his thoughts on the art of translation, Evelyn analyzes his own standards:

I have yet been as industrious as I could to explain the *Poets* sense and meaning in his own natural way; using very little *Paraphrase,* where I could possibly contract him without impeachment of his Argument, or defacing of the Ornament: so that if I have seldom exceeded the number of *Verses,* save where the *Rhyme* it self obliges me sometimes to multiply *Epithetes,* and protract the line; I have neither made a disadvantageous bargain for our *Language,* nor in the least violated the limits of an *Interpreter,* which are yet infinitely more indulgent, and give a far greater latitude, as I could abundantly exemplifie.

Putting these remarks into the context of seventeenth-century theory and practice of translation, one sees that Evelyn stands in a middle ground; he is firmly literal in his self-imposed standards but well aware of the freer forms of translation. He could scarcely have set himself a stricter goal, along with truth to the argument and "ornament," than line-by-line rendition, contracting the hexameters into heroic couplets. His cheerful admission of having padded out lines, as the rhyme demanded, presumes that the only objection to this would be the inexact correspondence with the vocabulary of the original. The thought of distortions of pronunciation or of rhythm troubled him little: "suppose I had now and then (as to my best notice I have no where) wrested a syllable unjustly, or adopted an illegitimate word, I had yet been no less excusable even by the verdict and indulgence of our Author, *'Multa novis verbis, praesertim cum sit agendum/Propter egestatem Linguae, & rerum novitatem.'*" But in fact, Lucretius is excusing only neologisms and says nothing of wresting syllables. All in all, Evelyn's remarks are an accurate description of his own method and a complacent statement of the conservative position on translating.

The translation itself is the least interesting part of the book. Scholars of Lucretius credit it with substantial accuracy, marred by occasional improvisations or misunderstandings.[6] It is no poem in its own right, but it does stand up as a readable versified translation. Evelyn's poetic diction is fairly conventional. His handling of the meter is not utterly inept. In comparing his and Dryden's translations, one finds his rhythms are considerably more irregular than Dryden's, a quality that in itself is fairly pleasing; but the frequency of the caesura is at least as great as Dryden's. The combination makes for a jerkiness quite out of harmony with the thought. As for rhyme, well might he have complained about what its exigencies meant to him. The obtrusiveness of expletives, awkward inversions, confusing syntax, and distorted pronunciations makes us more aware of manful struggles than of melody.

After the text come the "Animadversions," and the inadequacy of Evelyn's performance in this section is beyond dispute. The style is undistinguished, and the ideas are a muddle. The question is why Evelyn bothered with it at all. Reconstructing the event, one suspects that he started on the work with no thought that it would elicit criticism. When the commendatory prefaces contributed by his friends and relatives used such expressions for Lucretius as "morose" and "crabbed" and considered it a compliment to say "this Piece is The Taming of the Shrew. What shall I say More?," he apparently became uneasy. Moreover, when Evelyn mentioned to Jeremy Taylor, his spiritual adviser, that the work was in progress, Taylor expressed doubt of his prudence. Evelyn designed the "Animadversions," presumably, to correct the possible ill effects of Lucretius' errors and then at the last minute tried to suppress that section, evidently dissatisfied with his success as rebuttalist; but his publisher insisted that the essay was needed to fill out an otherwise skimpy book. In another letter to Taylor, Evelyn covered his disquiet with a cheerful tone and a bizarre simile, borrowed without explanation from Gassendi: "The captiue woman was in the old law to haue ben head-shauen, and her excraescencies pared off, before she was brought to the bed of her lord. I hope I haue so done with this author, as far as I have penetrated" (April 27, 1656).[7]

The significance of this book does not lie in the quality of Evelyn's performance. His uneasiness about the topic had lasting effects for himself: he did not ever again write about philosophy or even issue a corrected edition of Book I, let alone publish the remainder of his translation. Yet the very fact of his having chosen this work and published even the fraction that he did contributed markedly to the acceptance and popularizing of both Lucretius and Epicurus.

The elaborate full title of Evelyn's next book is self-descriptive: *The French Gardiner: Instructing how to Cultivate all sorts of Fruit-trees, & Herbs for the Garden: together with directions to dry & conserve them in their Natural, first written by R. D. C. D. W. B. D. N. and now transplanted into English by Philocepos,* 1658. The initials (in reverse order) refer to Nicolas de Bonnefons, the French author, who first published his *Le jardinier français* in 1651. Evelyn's fanciful pseudonym for himself, lover of gardens, made no real mystery of the translator since he signed the dedication in his own name.

In a preface to this book, Evelyn expressed the wish to become "the first propagator in England" (*Misc. Writ.,* 98); but in later editions he eliminated this interesting phrase. However, his love of gardening was lifelong. So, although this work is a translation, it has a double distinction in Evelyn's literary career: of being his first publication on this topic and of carrying a sketch of his projected writings on the whole range of gardening. The body of the work consists of four parts: two treatises, each over a hundred pages long, which discuss the handling of (1) trees and shrubs and (2) fruits and vegetables; a highly detailed catalogue of fruit trees around Paris; and an appendix on methods of preserving fruits.

A dozen seventeenth-century gardening books had already achieved notable circulation and reprinting, and Evelyn expressed some misgivings about whether his work was needed (97). But there were three printings the first year and four subsequent editions during his lifetime. In 1669, he wrote a new dedicatory epistle, referring to the reception given the work and his own opinion of it: "The success of the First Edition of this Book, has produced a second. . . . The character which I first adventur'd on this Piece, (when I boldly pronounc'd it for the very best that was extant on the subject) has been amply confirm'd by the suffrages of all who have since written upon it" (99). The tone of the diary entry at the time of publication suggests that it too may have been written, or amplified, after Evelyn saw how great was the demand for his book: "Now was published my *French Gardiner* the first & best of that kind that introduced the use of the *Olitorie* Garden to any purpose" (Dec. 6, 1659).

The one-page preface "To the Reader" (100) explains what portions of Bonnefons have been omitted. On the advice of a certain lady "who is a person of quality, and curious in" the art of preserving fruits with sugar, Evelyn has left out this material and turned the lady's judgment into a ponderous compliment, saying that in comparison with Bonnefons, "the fair sex . . . do infinitely exceed, whenever they please to divertise themselves in that *sweet* employment." His further reason for neglecting Bonnefons' writing on cookery is that "it is a mysterie that I am little acquainted withall . . . I have some experience in the Garden, and more divertisement, yet I have none in the shambles." "Some experience" is, of course, only a modestly conventional disclaimer. The preface claims that he did this work "to gratifie a noble friend, who had only that empire over me, as to make me quit some more serious employment for a few days in obedience to his command." If this was meant as literally as it sounds, the sentence throws light on the pace at which Evelyn worked: to translate an almost three-hundred page text in "a few days" would take steady application and driving energy.

In the dedication to Thomas Henshaw, Evelyn gives a sketch of his projected gardening work. Introducing the subject by saying that he had "long since had inclinations and a design of communicating some other things of this nature from my own experience; and especially, concerning the ornaments of gardens," he goes on to list these: "parterrs, grotts, fountains . . . perspectives, rocks, aviaries, vivaries, apiaries, pots, conservatories, piscinas, groves, cryptas, cabinets, ecchos . . ." (97–98). The project is untitled here, but in the fragmentary manuscript he called it *Elysium Britannicum.*

This first public reference to the *Elysium Britannicum* may serve as an occasion for surveying the history of this great unfinished work. Apparently this year of 1658 was when the plan really began to form in Evelyn's mind. He had already read and collected the notable books on gardening, both Classical and modern.[8] What he envisioned was a compendium of their ideas, together with information based on his own experience; and his outlines divided the entire work into three books. It was to start with the land and earth to be used for the garden, proceed to the design of gardens, and end with the details of the cultivation and use of the plants and their products. *The French Gardiner,* according to its dedicatory epistle, covered "the soyle, the situation, and the planting" (98). The scope was vast, but initially it was perhaps not impracticable.

In a letter to Thomas Browne, Evelyn gave a lengthy description of the whole: "our drift is a noble, princely, and universall Elysium, capable of all the amoenities that can naturally be introduced into gardens of pleasure." He invited Browne to be a contributor "in my philosophico-medicall garden . . . as likewise in my coronary chapter, and that of transmutations." Evelyn claimed that he had already finished more than half of the design "rudely." [9] A year later, Jeremy Taylor wrote Evelyn that he was looking forward to seeing "some parts & steps of your progression" with the thought of adding his own share "to your building, though but hair & stickes" (Feb. 10, 1660).

According to the Royal Society of London *Philosophical Transactions,* the work, "bearing the Title of *Englands Elysium*," was being prepared for printing by November 15, 1669; but it did not appear. In the same year, when the second edition of *The French Gardiner* was published, Evelyn rewrote the dedicatory epistle and omitted all reference to the *Elysium.* What was happening, apparently, was that the monumental undertaking was becoming self-defeating in its ambition. In 1679, Evelyn expressed discouragement: "I am almost out of hope that I shall ever have strength and leisure to bring it to maturity" (722).

By 1699, the work had become truly encyclopedic in range and impossible of fulfillment—for any one man, much less a man of seventy-nine. This year Evelyn published "The Plan of a Royal Garden," as he now entitled it; and each of the nine books on gardening which he had by now written covered but a small subdivision of the grand plan (730–32). At that rate, *Elysium Britannicum* would have been nearly fifty volumes. Along with the "Plan," Evelyn published his admission of defeat:

We have heard of one who studied and contemplated the nature of bees only, for sixty years; after which, you will not wonder, that a person of my acquaintance should have spent almost forty in gathering and amassing materials for an hortulan design, to so enormous an heap, as to fill some thousand pages. . . . But you may justly wonder, and condemn the vanity of it too, with that reproach, 'This man began to build, but was not able to finish!' This has been the fate of that undertaking. . . . But this is that which abortives the perfection of the most glorious and useful undertakings; the unsatiable coveting to exhaust all that should or can be said upon every head. (729)

This is indeed failure on a grand scale, and that is the note Evelyn struck. The grace and strength of his prose declare the victory of noble ambition, not the frustration of failure. And his tone of near complacency is echoed by historians of gardening and students of Evelyn's writings alike, who customarily cite the work or its various parts and almost always in tones of admiration.[10]

Usually Evelyn wrote in connection with some other activity or association in his daily life, although he generally did not mention this occasion or only referred to it briefly and formally. When, therefore, a really personal explanation appears in one of his writings, it impresses the reader rather more intensely than

[26]

might acknowledgments of similar emotions or experiences by less reticent authors.

One such exception is *The Golden Book of St. John Chrysostom, concerning the Education of Children, Translated out of the Greek,* 1659. The diary reference says that Evelyn "dedicated [it] to both my Brothers, to comfort them upon the losse of their Children" (Sept. 16, 1658); but, in the Epistle Dedicatory itself, he states that he had started the work "to mitigate and attemper the sorrowes which do still oppresse me, for the loss of my children, and especially of that *One* so precious to me" (105). Evelyn lost three children as infants, another at six years old, two more in their teens; only one of the eight outlived him. His elder brother George had eleven children die young out of fourteen; and Richard, the younger Evelyn brother, lost four—all sons— out of five. Among these, the most severe loss for John was his firstborn, Richard. The child had survived the hazards of infancy. He had begun to flourish as an extraordinarily precocious young-ster, "a child of most prodigious hopes" (Aug. 24, 1656), gifted intellectually and morally. When he succumbed at six, the au-topsy which his father ordered revealed a deformed liver and spleen. This boy was "that *One* so precious to me" alluded to in the Epistle Dedicatory (*Misc. Writ.*, 105), "the prettiest, and dearest Child, that ever parents had . . . for beauty of body a very Angel, & for endowments of mind, of incredible & rare hopes. . . . Here ends the joy of my life, & for which I go even mourning to the grave" (Jan. 27 and 30, 1658).

The one comfort Evelyn clung to, he says in the dedication, was the thought of "there being nothing capable truly to compose the mind of a good man for the absence of his friend or of his child, like the contemplation of his undoubted felicity" (106). That the boy merited a lasting reward, for both his intellectual and spir-itual qualities, Evelyn makes clear. He lists in detail his extraor-dinary accomplishments in languages (Latin, Greek, French, Ital-ian, and Dutch), the Classics, mathematics and geometry, and music (he played the organ). Both his mother and father were his tutors, but even more important perhaps was his self-instruc-tion. Only two hours of study a day were by Evelyn's command; the rest of the reading was at the boy's own option "without con-straint or the least severity, unseene, and totally imported by his own inclination" (109).

More extraordinary than these brilliant intellectual achieve-
ments, however, was the boy's spiritual development. A twentieth-century reader might not put the same interpretation as
Evelyn did upon such precocious piety, but one cannot doubt
that the picture is from life. Evelyn describes it with circumstantial vividness: little Richard's promptitude in arising; his frequent
times of prayer; his inducements to others to pray with him; his
benign tolerance of "his younger brother, with whose imperti-
nencies he would continually bear, saying he was but a child, and
understood no better"; his apposite quotations from the Scrip-
tures, the more unlikely for their being uttered by a fellow little
enough to be sitting on a visitor's knee "and, as we thought, not
minding the discourse"; his reiterations of "being weary of this
troublesome world"; and his pitiful anxieties on his deathbed that
perhaps he called too often on the name of God for ease and that
his prayers might be unacceptable since he found it hard to "hold
his hands out of bed in the posture of praying" (109–11). The
sketch reads more like a nineteenth-century novel than a real-life
story and is a valuable document for its time, even presuming that
young Richard was not a typical child. Evelyn's selection of details and his own tone of wonder produce a character sketch
which cannot be read with indifference.

Richard's education was not based on Chrysostom, Evelyn tells
his reader; and a brief note explains that the first time the text was
printed was in 1656 in Paris. Probably one of the reasons why the
work appealed to Evelyn was that Chrysostom, though not an
easygoing pedagogue, outlines a more temperate formation of
the child than that countenanced for young Richard. The title
generally assigned to Chrysostom's work is "Concerning Vainglory and Liberal Education." An address to wealthy parents, it
first examines the evils of vainglory and then presents and analyzes education as the way to obviate this fault. Evelyn, omitting
the entire part on vainglory, starts where Chrysostom turns to
education specifically. So abrupt is Chrysostom's own transition
that this omission causes no obscurity; in fact, Evelyn's essay has
a much tighter unity than the original.

Chrysostom's language is specific, imagistic, and concrete; and
his tone is maturely authoritative. These features lend themselves
readily to translation. A Chrysostom scholar calls Evelyn's work
"far from accurate. He sometimes slides over difficult passages . . .

sometimes he makes palpable errors," but he also notes that "Evelyn's version is distinguished by the dignity and literary skill that one would expect from its author." [11] Evelyn's errors do not distort the general sense of the address, and much is added by his own pleasing rhythms, pointed inversions, and carefully emphasized parallel constructions.

Taken together, Evelyn's dedicatory epistle and Chrysostom's text produce an effect of general homogeneity with some marked contrasts. Both men assume the urgency of a sound educative plan and the same values. But, where Evelyn is intensely emotional and personal, Chrysostom is dispassionate and entirely impersonal. Contrarily, where Evelyn greatly admires an austere otherworldliness, Chrysostom sets his sights lower and has an eye for the practicable. The prefatory material looks to the past—the devastation of the new generation of the family; but the reason for translating Chrysostom's essay lies in the belief that other Evelyns will replace those who have died. Yet this optimism does not deny the anguish of the hour; Evelyn closes the Epistle Dedicatory: "my tears mingle so fast with my inke, that I must break off here, and be silent" (111). The tension between sorrow and hope, austerity and moderation, personal expression and detachment gives a unique character to the work.

Individual as are the occasion and expression of Evelyn's *Golden Book,* the work shows too that he more or less deliberately associated it with two significant literary traditions: the eulogistic epistle and the courtesy book.

He notes explicitly his precedent for the form of the dedication. Having described the virtue of his son and completed his account of his death, he adds, "Deare Brothers, indulge me these excesses. It is not a new thing which I doe. St. Hierom wrote divers Epistles, which he inscribed his Epitaphs; and never was a Paula or Estochium dearer to him then this your nephew was" (111). As an early Church Father, like Chrysostom, Jerome was an appropriate authority to cite and to provide Evelyn with an example for his literary economy in having the one preface serve as dedicatory epistle and eulogy.

Of the many spiritual texts to choose from for a translation, Evelyn picked one which gives great emphasis to the social order. Thus, his text is properly associated with the genre of courtesy literature. This type of writing, which had as great a vogue in

Renaissance England as in Italy where it mainly originated, traditionally addressed itself to the aristocracy as it surveyed the education, accomplishments, and manners of a gentleman. Morals came into the early courtesy books but largely as background for their secular consequences. Chrysostom's essay similarly, while presuming supernatural goals as the ultimate ones, aims at producing a Christian who is a true gentleman. Evelyn, by his choice of vocabulary, brings his version directly into the conduct-book tradition, as a comparison of a twentieth-century translation with Evelyn's reveals.[12] Wherever the modern translation uses "athlete," Evelyn says "champion": the frequently repeated goal is to make "a Champion for Christ." The modern speaks of "a strict tutor to direct the boy"; Evelyn has "a diligent tutor, who may compose and regulate his manners." The modern uses the word "righteously" where Evelyn says "to perfection." For "exercise this child's soul in virtue," Evelyn has "cultivate their minds." In each instance, Evelyn's language is distinctly that of the courtesy tradition; for he is speaking of the whole man or of his manners rather than concentrating on his morals.

Thus, in both choice of text and treatment, Evelyn aligned his work firmly with books of manners and, one may observe, with the shifting trend in this genre. His theological presumptions do not bear the mark of Puritanism, which was to become common in eighteenth-century courtesy books; but in almost every other respect he anticipates the innovations of eighteenth-century courtesy literature—its practicality, the simplicity of teaching techniques, the emphasis on the Bible rather than on the Classics, an ethical rather than a spiritual preoccupation, and its moral strenuousness.

III A Character of England

Abruptly abandoning the business of translation which had occupied him for several years, Evelyn produced in 1659 one of his most original and literary works, A Character of England, a satirical character sketch of his nation at mid-century. In letter form, a fictitious Frenchman gives his noble patron an account of a "hasty and desultory peregrination" in England (148). The patron is visualized as himself knowing England, as not wanting any political commentary, but as seeking the personal reactions of his correspondent. Evelyn establishes this pretense in a preface to the reader. Remaining anonymous, he claims that "this severe piece" in French, by an unknown author, chanced into his hands. As a loyal Englishman, he at first resolved to suppress so shameful an exposé. But he has had second thoughts, for some reformation might come of such instruction.

The technique of inventing a foreign traveler through whose eyes national idiosyncrasies are seen is familiar to the student of satire. Most accounts of the development of this satiric convention start with Giovanni Paolo Marana's six-volume work, *The Turkish Spy* in 1684, but Evelyn antedates this work by twenty-five years. Evelyn does not present an admittedly assumed persona, as Montesquieu and Goldsmith were to do in the following century; an acknowledged masquerade was probably unimaginable for him and would have seemed self-defeating. But it is not the presence or absence of pretense that makes the imaginary foreign visitor a successful medium of satire. Evelyn put his finger on the essence of the device, to force the reader to see himself as others see him. He maintains this effect throughout by his astonishment at things English and by constant comparisons with France.

A Character of England starts with a semblance of plan, the traveler's own itinerary: the arrival at Dover, the trip to London, and first impressions of the metropolis, particularly of the buildings. Since churches are among the architectural interests, the letter has some logic in examining next "the several worships" found in London (152). But this examination is so extended, constituting perhaps a fifth of the entire essay, that it is more a digression, as the author himself admits. He returns to his ramble about the London streets, only to stray indoors again, this time to the taverns. This introduces the English drinking habits. Hereupon, the author abandons his ambulatory design and simply ranges over his impressions and recollections of society in a series of sketches and anecdotes, with related comments on manners, fashion, terms of address, conversation, social affairs, and the pleasure gardens of the day. The essay closes with a flurry of miscellaneous observations. All in all, the looseness of the organization suggests naturalness and spontaneity. So does the alternation, throughout the essay, of generalization, specific detail, typical example, and personal comment. The visitor is keenly observant and generous with his reported facts.

Evelyn provides many interesting details about church practices. He describes the canting tone used by preachers, the thick
velvet cushions on which the preachers loll while giving the sermon, and the vagaries, among the male congregation, as to
when to be hatted and when bareheaded. He reports that
churches were kept locked except on Sunday and that not only
were organs banned from the churches but they were transferred
to taverns where the trade chanted their "bestiall bacchanalias"
thus accompanied (158). At times, the sharpness of the satiric
viewpoint produces rhetorical outbursts. St. Paul's is a "goodly
and venerable fabrick" but so horrendously abused and in such
vile surroundings that the traveller exclaims, "O! how loathsome a
Golgotha" (151). Expressing regret for the many religious practices no longer observed, he writes epigrammatically, "the religion
of England is preaching and sitting on Sundaies" (153). As for
the creed and the commandments, "this is milke for babes and
they are all giants," he says with heavy irony (155).

His social documentation ranges over many of the London
scenes. He tells of the sudden proliferation of alehouses and the
custom for women of quality to frequent these places. He mentions the frequency of fires, seven years before the Great Fire.
He describes the effect of the new fuel, sea coal; its strench, heavy
residue, and respiratory consequences; and the production of
smog such that he has been "in a spacious church where I could
not discern the minister for the smoak." So overwhelmed is London by this abomination that, "if there be a resemblance of hell
upon earth, it is in this volcano in a foggy day" (157). He describes the London parks, especially Spring Garden, new at the
time, where it was not forbidden for young company to stay as late
as midnight, amidst thickets of a density "contrived to all advantages of gallantry" (165). In restaurants, he notes that the English refuse to bargain for their meals, considering this French
habit "a piece of frugality beneath them" (166). His dismay at
the mad speed on the highways produces one of the many epigrams in the essay when he exclaims, "All the coaches in London
seem to drive for midwives" (167).

Evelyn anatomizes with similar precision the social behavior of
the aristocrats. At social gatherings, the custom is that healths be
drunk to all present; consequently, drunkenness is almost inevi-
table, even in the presence of ladies. One extreme group, im-

pecunious sons of wealthy families "who stile themselves Hectors" (160), are given to such entertainments as drinking their own blood at a revel and becoming highwaymen to finance their dissipations. Gambling at cards is no longer restricted to men. Sumptuary laws are not enforced: chambermaids wear lace and silk just like their betters; elderly ladies wear colors. Women call men by their first names. Dancing masters are received socially, mix freely at balls, and gain great wealth by their trade. Formal visits last much longer than in France, yet conversation is far inferior. The English custom is for all to stay at table until the last has finished eating, whereas in France each withdraws at his own pace.

The features of English life which the visitor finds to approve are few, impersonal, and quickly noted: "the verdure of the country and delicious downes" (167), the bowling greens and race courses, the horses and deer, and the deer parks. His is the satirist's proper single-mindedness.

A Character of England is considered as a character of a country and its people, a form which combines genuine character writing with traditional rhetorical exercises describing national groups or institutions. Ideally, such a character should isolate the essence of the people described. Evelyn came as close to defining his subject as did most practitioners of this type of writing. His book is further associated with character writing by the fact that it contains several small character sketches, most notably the rather vivid and pithy descriptions of the Presbyterians and the Independents.

Evelyn ably hit the right tone for his work: there is an immediacy of response that rings true and a helter-skelter tumble of impressions that would be characteristic of a quick tour. So acute is his eye for idiosyncrasies, so natural are his reactions, so vivid his sketches, that it is hard to believe that it was written by a man who had not been out of England for six or seven years. In fact, it is very possible that Evelyn wrote the book as early as 1650: the evidence is inconclusive.

The work was a success. There were three editions in the first year, a French translation, a reprinting in the eighteenth century, and three reprintings in the nineteenth century. Additional testimony to its impact is that it called forth a formal reply, *Gallus Castratus, an Answer to a Slanderous Pamphlet, called the Char-*

acter of England, 1659, which debates twelve of Evelyn's criticisms. The tone and language are vituperative, and the approach is more one of name-calling than of debate. Evelyn answered with "A Letter in Vindication of this 'Character,' against the Sordid Reproaches of 'Gallus Castratus,' " which he affixed to the third edition. This letter has two distinct literary interests: its use of acid language and its presentation of a defense of satire.

For one who normally expressed himself with utmost civility, Evelyn shows extraordinary gusto and imagination in his use of invective. Even while deploring it as a satiric weapon, he says that he must use it with such an opponent as "this scorpion," "scabbed sheep," "the offspring of Billings-gate" (144–45). Alluding to the title of his adversary's attack, he produces as an inspired finale in this string of epithets, "this whiffling capon-maker" (146). He imputes therapeutic power to satire, almost sanctimoniously deplores those who reject criticism, and then with surprisingly vivid diction cries out, "But thus the urinall is cast into the physitians face" (145).

Less startling is Evelyn's discussion of satire. He appeals to Classical authority; prescribes moderation in manner and language; and stresses the moral function of satire, describing *A Character* as "charitably shewing us our avowed deformities, and the expedients to redresse them." He says that he heard "a learned and sober preacher quote the 'Character' in his sermon, and reproach the people for their irreverent behaviour in the church in the very language of that book" (144). Yet, routine as its ideas seem, the work was original in this respect: it is one of the very first examples in English literature of such a defense and in fact one of the rare pieces of formal literary criticism written before the Restoration. Indeed, *A Character of England* is one of Evelyn's most witty, imaginative, literary, and influential books.

IV *First Political Pamphlets*

Evelyn's career as a political writer began late in 1659 with *An Apologie for the Royal Party: Written in a Letter to a Person of the late Councel of State. By a Lover of Peace and of his Countrey: with a Touch at the pretended Plea for the Army.*[13] Richard Cromwell's inadequacies had become evident early in this year, and the Royalists' hopes began to revive. In this pamphlet, Evelyn made a strong argument for the restoration of the king.

The immediate occasion was a pamphlet called *The Army's Plea for Their Present Practice,* justifying the army's having taken over the government in mid October. Within ten days, apparently totally on his own initiative, Evelyn wrote and published a reply. His satisfaction in the work is evident from the diary entry: "[Nov.] 7 Was published my bold *Apologie* for the *King,* in this time of danger, when it was capital to speake or write in favour of him; It was twice printed, so universaly it tooke." The courage required in the face of the real risk involved was apparently considerable, even though the work was anonymous as to its author, publisher, and the person addressed. This addressee has since been identified as Colonel Herbert Morley, a friend of Evelyn's and an official of both the Parliament and the army, to whom Evelyn appealed by letter and in person, as well as in this anonymous publication. Morley disappointed Evelyn in not strongly supporting the restoration of the king, but subsequent events suggest that Evelyn's intervention may have played a part in hastening and easing the return of the monarchy. In fourteen tightly written pages, Evelyn denounces the tyranny of the rebels; shows something of the calamities they have brought on the nation; offers a glowing picture of the integrity of Charles, the royal prince; and compares the benefits of reform and restoration with the horrors that will result from further resistance.

Besides the urgency of the topic, the essay is also distinguished by a style which persuasively communicates Evelyn's own heartfelt commitment to the cause. The tone is authoritative, and Evelyn spares his opponents nothing in his denunciations. His language is elegant, the text is filled with biblical allusions, and he makes frequent use of strongly parallel structure and of rhetorical questions. With resounding scorn he asks, "What is become of this ignorant and furious zeal, this pretence of an universall perfection in the Religious and the Secular, after all that blood and Treasure, Rapine and Injustice, which has been exhausted, and perpetrated by these sons of Thunder? Where is the King, whom they swear to make so glorious, but meant it in his *Martyrdome?* Where is the classis [a governing body in reformed churches], and the Assembly, the Lay-elder; all that geare of Scotish disci-

pline, and the fine new Trinkets of Reformation?" (2). He writes
here with true rhetorical power.

Sometimes he speaks of the general situation: "to what condition you have already reduced this once flourishing kingdom,
since all has been your own, let the intollerable oppressions, taxes,
Excises, sequestrations, confiscations, plunders, customes, decimations, not to mention the plate, even to very thimbles and the
bodkins (for even to these did your avarice descend) and other
booties, speak" (4). At other times, he cites individual abuses,
for instance, censuring the treatment of Stafford: "Under the Sun
was it never heard, that a man should be condemned for transgressing no law, but that which was made after the fact, and
abrogated after execution" (4). He varies lengthy sentences with
rapid-fire factual reporting. A whole sequence of names of various rebels who met disgraceful deaths concludes thus: "*Ireton*
perished of the Plague, and *Hoyle* hanged himself; *Staplie* died
mad, and *Cromewell* in a fit of rageing; and if there were any
others worthy the taking notice of, I should give you a list of
their names and of their destinies" (5).

Evelyn is rather more successful in his damnings than in his
praises, although some of his defense of Charles is fairly incisive.
But, when he starts exalting him, the phrases seem less ideally
suited to his subject: "For his vertues and Morality, I provoak the
most refined Family in this Nation to produce me a Relation of
more piety and moderation" (10). If ever Evelyn looked back to
this pamphlet in after years, this description must have caused
him some chagrin. But, in all other respects, *An Apology* was a
distinguished start of his political writing.

With the frustration of his hopes that Morley would act, Evelyn's direct involvement in the Restoration ceased; and, in February, 1660, he fell seriously ill. For almost two months he was
confined to bed, and he witnessed only remotely the triumphant
reversal of the Royalist fortunes. But the moment his strength began to return, he resumed his part, again by means of political
writing. The diary gives an unusually full account of the event:

During this Sicknesse came innumerable of my Relations & friends to
visite me, and it retarded my going into the Country longer than I
intended: however I writ, and printed a letter in defence of his
Majestie against a wicked forged paper, pretended to be sent from
Bruxells, to defame his Majesties person, Virtues, & render him odi-

ous, now when every body were in hopes & expectation of the Gen:
& Parliaments recalling him & stablishing the Government on its
antient and right basis: In doing which towards the decline of my
sicknesse, & setting-up long in my bed, had caused a small relapse.
(Feb. 17—Apr. 5, 1660)

Evelyn entitled his pamphlet *The Late News or Message from
Bruxels Unmasked, & His Majesty Vindicated,* since the "wicked
forged paper" to which he was replying was called *Newes from
Brussels, In a Letter from a neer Attendant on His Majesties Person to a Person of Honour here; which casually became thus publique.*[14] Needless to say, both works appeared anonymously. But
in Evelyn's pamphlet, the publisher's name is given: the return-
ing security for defenders of the king is apparent.

Evelyn makes three main points. He "unmasks" the author, in
the sense of showing that he is not a near attendant on the king
but a paid writer for the Commonwealth party; therefore, he
does not speak with firsthand authority, as he claims. Evelyn then
attacks as false the charges against Charles: that Charles is re-
vengeful and anti-Presbyterian. His answer to these is ultimately
just a firm and repeated denial. And, finally, he expatiates on
Charles's virtues, suggesting that such a man could never take
reprisals as predicted in *News from Brussels.*

The rebuttal is given sharp focus by Evelyn's technique of bor-
rowing words and phrases and of reapplying them wittily. The
more incisive or ridiculous images particularly catch his attention. For instance, the rebel writes, "he is an asse that angles and
hides not his hooks" (*Misc. Writ.,* 197) and then claims that he
has seen through the Royalists' scheme which will encourage the
Presbyterians to destroy the more fanatical sects and thus save
the Royalists the trouble: "thus half the beard they shave themselves, let us alone with t'other: drown first the kittlings, let the
dam that litter'd them alone a little longer" (199). Evelyn takes
these images and ideas and turns them back upon the rebel author: "Sir, your nets are seen, and your fallacies fail you; the
hooks you mention are laid too visibly; the fish you would catch
are so far from swallowing, they will not bite at all; you were
best therefore go shave your own beard, as you have those in
your letter, and your scull too; and if your brain prove not
thence more pregnant, 'twill serve (however) to stuffe your

powch instead of what such your angels were intended to have holpen you to" (200)—that is, the money paid for this pamphlet.

In another example, the anonymous author uses the phrase "Plantaginet's in pickle" (198), meaning that Charles is just biding his time for the day of revenge for his exile. Evelyn picks up the expression and describes the entire pamphlet as "false fictions of a son of Belial, which will remain in pickle to arise up against this forger at a tribunal, where the offspring of a Plantagenet, whose most innocent blood he hath sucked, will bring in a record ... which will fright his guilty soul down to that place of horrour prepared for him and his fellow Regicides" (199).

A large measure of the impact of Evelyn's work derives from the reader's knowing the other pamphlet. Read with that, Evelyn's has a quality of sparring and of repartee and a consequent vitality which is lessened without the contrast. Beyond that, what mark the style of *The Late News from Brussels Unmasked* are a few original phrases, Evelyn's usual intense earnestness, the dignity of his tone in opposition to irresponsible attacks, and a rather rambling presentation which is not incoherent only because the whole work is so short. The pamphlet is generally considered a successful piece of polemic writing.

Before we conclude this first decade of Evelyn's literary career, one other publication of 1660 requires a word. An anonymous translation appeared in that year, *The Manner of Ordering Fruit-trees* by Sieur Le Gendre, which most likely was Evelyn's work. He owned the French original, *De la manière de cultiver les arbres fruitiers* (Paris, 1652); and there are markings in his copy which may have been made incidental to the work of making this translation. The general style and diction of the translation are like Evelyn's, and the subject was of the sort that attracted him. The evidence is not conclusive but is generally accepted.[15]

In these first ten years of Evelyn's writing for publication, we see great dependence and also distinct originality. Translations make up the bulk of his production, but Evelyn selected these freely and imaginatively and showed literary awareness in his introductions. His original works of this period are modest efforts, not startling as to occasion, ideas, or style; but they are carefully fashioned and were well received.

CHAPTER 2

1661-1664—For King and Royal Society

THE next four years were the most prolific of Evelyn's literary career. His own maturity, a large measure of domestic as well as national tranquillity, and the generally revitalized activities in the arts played their part in this fertility. But two other forces very directly stimulated Evelyn at this time: the Royal Society and his Royal Highness, Charles II.

I *"Pico Teneriffe";* A Panegyric to Charles the Second

The group soon to become officially entitled the Royal Society, which had been meeting in a very loosely organized way for some years, rapidly took firm shape in 1660 and Evelyn was promptly attracted. In January, 1661, he was named a fellow; in March, he delivered a report as part of an investigation which the society had been conducting on the island of Teneriffe in the Canaries, having gathered his information from English merchants who had journeyed there in 1646. Evelyn's speech was not printed then, but some years later it appeared in modified form in Thomas Sprat's *History of the Royal Society* (1667) as "A Relation of the Pico Teneriffe in the Great Canaries, Receiv'd from some considerable Merchants and Men worthy of Credit, who went to the top of it."

Evelyn gives the impression of being little more than a scribe in this report, for he uses the first-person plural in presenting the material. He describes the climb, the summit, a grotto visited, the island in general and its flora and fauna, and a kind of mummifying burial practice found there. Two curious skills of the natives get special attention: ear-splitting whistles allegedly audible at five miles and techniques for pole-jumping off rocks of sixty-foot heights. In respect to the latter, the account adds, "Their novices sometimes break their necks in learning" (213).

In April, the long-awaited crowning of the king took place. For

the occasion, Evelyn wrote a piece which he presented personally to King Charles. While the king accepted it graciously, his
anticipatory remarks suggest that he had had his fill of encomi-
ums, for he "had asked if the panegyric was in Latin and 'hoped
it would not be very long.'"[1] It is, in fact, short—sixteen pages of
unrelieved enthusiasm, entitled *A Panegyric to Charles the Second, presented to his Majestie the XXIII of April, being the Day
of his Coronation,* 1661. Pious recollections of the martyred king,
the period of exile, the unaltered devotion of the people, the
king's return and clemency, the restoration of law and order, and
the king's personal abilities and virtues—these are the topics. The
elaboration is in the form of rhapsodic flights.

"Great Prince," "your sacred Majesty," "a true Phoenix," "O
best Idea of Princes" are some of the titles Evelyn uses to address
Charles. Likening him to "that blessed Martyr" his father, Evelyn
pictures Charles II as "rising from those Sacred Ashes Testator
and Heir; Father and yet Son; Another, and yet the same; intro-
suming as it were his Spirit, as he breath'd it out" (6). Celebrat-
ing the Restoration itself, Evelyn writes, "Miraculous Reverse! O
marvel greater than Mans Counsel! who will believe that which
his eyes do see? . . . our Churches, Tribunals, Theaters, Palaces,
lift up their heads again; the very fields do laugh and exalt. O
happy, and blessed spring!" (4) No techniques are spared: extended lists; carefully balanced constructions; allusion and quotation, in Latin and English; aureate and other rare diction; hyperbolic images; and endless rhetorical questions and exclamations.

Although Evelyn's main business was enumerating the king's
merits, he was not totally blind to his own interests in *A Panegyric.* He devotes a paragraph to thanking the king for his atten-
tions to "our Society [the Royal Society] at Greshham Colledge"
(14), and the passage is both a plea for continued support and
an eloquent piece of publicity. Evelyn expresses the bright hope
that this "Illustrious Assembly . . . may improve practical and
Experimental knowledge, beyond all that has been hitherto attempted, for the Augmentation of Science, and universal good of
Man-kind." The commendation was acknowledged by the Royal
Society with public thanks.

II Fumifugium; *"A Narrative"*

Concern for the health of the king—to say nothing of the London citizenry—and his researches at the Royal Society combined to produce his next work, *Fumifugium: or the Inconveniencie of the Aer and Smoak of London Dissipated.* Long disturbed by the problem, Evelyn tells in the dedication to the king that what bestirred him into print was the recent sight at Whitehall, where the king resided, of "a presumptious smoake issuing from one or two tunnels . . . to such a degree, as men could hardly discern one another for the clowd, and none could support, without manifest inconveniency" (*Misc. Writ.*, 207). He presented the work to the king in September, and a fortnight later he spent the day on the royal yacht: among other pastimes "his *Majestie* was pleasd to discourse to me about my Book inveing against the nuisance of the Smoke of Lond" (Oct. 1, 1661).

From the outset, Evelyn's tone is righteously indignant and pleasantly authoritative, and the presentation is neatly organized in three unequal parts. He first describes and denounces the extent and effects of the smoke menace in London; this subject takes up more than half the work. In the second part, he proposes the removal from London of those businesses which he considered most polluting. In the last section he gives a brief, second proposal for ameliorating the air by certain types of "fragrant and odoriferous" plantings (240).

Within these well-ordered divisions, Evelyn is still systematic, but not perfectly so. With almost overdone logic, he defines pure air, describes its effects on behavior, argues its importance, asserts its possibility especially in London's ideal location, and finally isolates the chief cause of the trouble—sea coal. He establishes that it is the industrial, not the domestic, use that matters. Then he itemizes in detail the pernicious effects of sea coal on health, property, and the beauty of the city. After that, his reasoning becomes somewhat obfuscated itself, as he circles anxiously about discussing the poisonous nature of sea coal, the excessive mortality rate in London, and the filth of the city.

Parts II and III are orderly but not totally single-minded. Part II gets so enthusiastic in its clean sweep of the atmosphere that it suddenly proposes a kind of wholesale renovation; churchyards, chandlers, butchers, prisons, and jails are to be packed out of town along with the brewers, dyers, lime-burners, salt and soap boilers, and other air polluters. Similarly, in Part III, where the subject is properly sweetbriar, jasmine, gillyflowers, and wild thyme, Evelyn suddenly discusses in the last paragraph how satisfactory it would be if slums could be prohibited.

The work abounds with ideas, and two are of particular interest to students of literature. One is the effect of air upon human behavior. The question of the relation between climate and personality, perhaps most famously set forth by Milton, was very popular in the seventeenth century. Evelyn's focus on air is more specific, but it is part of the whole physiopsychological theory. The other is the curious notion "that the purest Aers are soonest infected" (225); hence, smoke-laden air is a protection against plague. This type of antithesis was an admired image of the day, as in Shakespeare's line "Lilies that fester smell far worse than weeds." But where the poets use the contrast as a persuasive natural symbol, Evelyn treats the theory as a sophistical paradox, proposed by men who want to sharpen their wits, and he gives other recondite examples: "for so Favorinus of old, and Menapius since, commended a quartan ague; Pirckhemierus the gout; Gutherius celebrated blindnesse . . ." (229–30).

One of the charms of Evelyn's essays at their best is the tumble of ideas that pours out of him when he begins to concentrate on any one subject. Listing the destructive effects of sea-coal smoke, pinpointing the chimneys in London that offend the most, and following the circulation of the blood as it conveys the smoke poisons into the whole body of man, he gives the impression that the ideas are coming to him in a quantity and with a rapidity that he can scarcely cope with. The poisonous effects of sea coal brings to his mind manifold and various reports of people who have, by small dosages, accustomed themselves to tolerate other kinds of poisons. Having proposed the removal of the trades out of London, he suddenly views an ever-widening prospect of advantages: the swamp air, on the riverbank below Greenwich where the trades will relocate, will be dried out by the smoke; business will prosper for the watermen who will transport the products to London; bankside land will be available for new buildings. When he considers whether there is a precedent for such a parliamentary action, he rapidly recalls not only English law but Jewish practices, a relevant custom "in the Spanish great towns of America," and "the *lex carnaria* of the Romans" (237).

The luxuriance of Evelyn's ideas derives in part from his reading. He quotes from or cites Diogenes, Anaximenes, Plato, Hippocrates, Avicenna, Vitruvius, Virgil, Claudian, Ovid, Lucan, Cicero, Erasmus, Heinsius, Kenelm Digby, Barclay. Intermingled with the learned sources are homely proverbs, curious facts, and commonplaces. Through spontaneous associations of ideas, he easily assimilates these references, and his style bears little trace of the pedant.

Harmonizing with this combination of strange facts and authoritative tone is Evelyn's use of rare words. "Septentrion," "imbelles," "antiperistasis," "clowed," "internunce," "alexipharmac," "fuliginous," "spiracles," "funest," "assuefaction," "tabid," "halitus," "inspissation" are some of the more memorable. The effects of his Latin reading are evident. Generally, he employs his vocabulary with little self-consciousness. One exception occurs in a description of a jocular plan to have "a vessel fraight with peel'd onions . . . attract the pollution of the aer and sail away with the infection to the sea"; chuckling over "this excellent conceit," Evelyn writes, "transportation of diseases we sometimes read of amongst the magneticall, or rather magical cures; but never before of this way of transfretation" (239).

The response to *Fumifugium* has been a consistent mixture of enthusiasm and inertia. That is, from the time of its publication through the several editions in this century, it has received respect and praise; but it produced scarcely any results of a practical order. According to the diary, Evelyn prepared at the king's command a bill along the lines outlined in the book, but there is no record that it was ever brought before Parliament. Possibly the limetrees in St. James's Park were the result of Evelyn's suggestion of fragrant plantings.

The recognition given the work was sufficient to win Evelyn a place in an anonymous verse satire on the Royal Society. Composed probably in 1663, "The Ballad of Gresham College" devoted several stanzas to *Fumifugium*. After describing Evelyn's attack on sea coal, the ballad says,

> Lett none att Fumifuge be scoffing
> Who heard att Church our Sundaye's Coughing.
> For melioration of the Ayre

Both for our Lungs and eke our noses,
To plant the Fields he doth take care
With Cedar, Juniper and Roses,
. . . .
O blessed witt that thus contrives
By new found out but facile Arte.
In pleasure to lengthen out our lives.
To teach us next to perfume —
And without fuell or smoake make fire
Some other Member will aspire.[2]

Southey wrote of Evelyn as a kind of tribute, "Satire, from whom nothing is sacred, scarcely attempted to touch him while living." [3] But satire can be a tribute of sorts, and the rather puerile verses quoted above are an acknowledgment that Evelyn, though no scientist himself, was regarded as a distinguished member of the Royal Society. Moreover, at the time of the Great Fire, many of Evelyn's warnings about the dangerous conditions of the city were proved justified, and he recorded that "the invective I but a little before dedicated to his Majestie . . . was lookd on as prophetic" (Sept. 5, 1666). When a fuel shortage was suffered in 1667, Evelyn was one of those officially consulted for solutions.

Subsequent reprintings and articles about *Fumifugium* combine respect for Evelyn with a touch of patronage. Evelyn's venerable reputation makes his a good name to enlist in the cause against air pollution until the present day. The antiquity of the work underlines the longevity of the problem. Each time *Fumifugium* has been reprinted, a new introduction points out that, far from measures having been taken, the situation has become worse. Evelyn complained that the trees in the city were without fruit, by the eighteenth century they were without leaves, and by the twentieth century not only fruit and leaf but trees as well are gone. Evelyn's estimate of the seriousness of the problem was unique in his time and without equal for over two hundred years. While his specific correctives continue to be ignored or treated as quaint and whimsical, the book has appeal for the modern reader. This derives from his genteel humanism, the earnestness of his pleas, and the tempering of these with unexpected elements of humor. The work is genuinely literary.

On the same boat ride during which there was the royal discussion of *Fumifugium,* the king assigned Evelyn his next writing project. Jealousy over precedence at state functions had been building up between the French and Spanish ambassadors and had produced a genuine skirmish at an official reception on September 30. The king was accused by some of partiality, and Evelyn's task was "vindication of his Majestie & carriage of his Officers, & standersby" (Oct. 1–3, 1661). The diary relates in unusually full detail the steps in composition of this brief piece which in manuscript carries the title *A Narrative of the Encounter between the French and Spanish Embassadors.* Evelyn tells of the king's command given him on Tuesday, October 1, and of his gathering the facts for a draft of the narrative, ready Wednesday. He was clearly dazzled by the king's uncommon courtesies in an interview on Thursday when, amid distractions, Evelyn read his narrative aloud "to his majesties greate satisfaction" and was given instructions for the final draft. On Friday morning the king had a conversation with the French ambassador "who it seemes had palliated the matter, & was very tame." On Saturday a re-writing was completed by Evelyn, further edited by the king, and finally delivered. That night Evelyn "slip'd home, being my selfe much indisposs'd & harass'd, with going about, & setting up to write, &c:"

There is no evidence that the *Narrative* was printed or published, as the king had said it would be, until 1665 when it appeared, abridged to about half its original length. The only significant difference in the abridged version is that it even more clearly vindicates the English bystanders at the reception. The original dwells for a lengthy paragraph on who threw brickbats; the printed text firmly states "that they were not cast by any of the *English,* is attested by the general consent of all the Spectators." [4]

Evelyn's narrative shows how bloody a business it was: various missiles were loosed, horses were hamstrung, forty men were wounded, some slain, to say nothing of the fact that the Franco-Hispanic peace was severely threatened. Evelyn's treatment is clear, circumstantial, fast-moving, and dispassionate. The king's command elicited a reportorial style which is brisker and more to the point than is usual for Evelyn.

III *Of Libraries and Fashions*

Evelyn's fifth work of 1661, which appeared not very long after the ambassadorial skirmish, had its origins in Paris in 1644. For in that year was published one of the most important seventeenth-century books about libraries, Gabriel Naudé's *Advis pour dresser une bibliotheque.* Evelyn was attracted to the book because of his own bibliomania and because Naudé's study was distinguished among the perhaps only a dozen then available on the subject. In the fall of 1661, Evelyn published a translation of the *Advis,* entitled *Instructions Concerning Erecting of a Library.* The translation includes the complete text, prefatory material, and table of contents. The titles of the chapters show its scope: why one ought to be curious in erecting libraries; how to get advice on the subject; the number of books needed; the proper quality and condition of books; the expedients by which they may be procured; where they should be kept; the order of arrangement; the ornamentation and decoration of the books and the library. The final statements, nominally on the scope and end of a library, are really on the staff—"well stipendiated"; the rules—liberty, regulated "with civility"; the catalogues—one by subject and one by author; and the stipulations for circulation.

The appeal of the work is in Naudé's ideas. His experience is everywhere evident: "a perfect Maxime, that there is no Book whatsoever, be it never so bad or decried, but may in time be sought for by some person or other" (20). He shows good sense when he points out that difficulty in locating a book does not really enhance its value or that just having vast numbers of books does not give a library lustre. He is practical; the quickest way to get a library is to buy someone else's. He is not above such homely advice as how often to place new books on the shelves and how often to dust. He is first and last a scholar: he wants tapestries on the walls for their insulation but cares nothing for elaborate floors and ceilings or for statuary in the library; he has no respect for the prestige that books can give; and his only interest in bindings regards their durability.

Pleasing as Naudé's ideas are, the same may not be said for his style, and Evelyn unfortunately made no effort to compensate for it. Naudé's nonstop sentences are like a caricature of bookishness. With some subordination but more often with loose coordination or the apposition of large elements, Naudé strings together seventy-five to a hundred words, rarely fewer and often more. Evelyn's translation, which is almost slavishly exact, if not always accurate, is very different from his handling of the La Mothe le Vayer and the Chrysostom. Perhaps this was a hasty job or perhaps Evelyn fell under the spell of Naudé's turgidity. The style is not a barrier to comprehension, and now and then there is a graceful phrase; but, in general, the effect is ponderous.

Once again Evelyn used the dedication as an occasion to praise the Royal Society and to explain its work. What is of historic moment is that in this dedicatory epistle he coined the name "Royal Society," which eventually was adopted for that group "of *Gentlemen,* and Refined Spirits that are universally *Learn'd,* that are *Read, Travell'd, Experienc'd* and Stout."

Evelyn's translation of Naudé had several practical results. So highly respected was the work that Evelyn himself was considered an authority on libraries. He reports in his diary being called on to evaluate distinguished book collections and to give advice about libraries. The late seventeenth century was a time of great expansion of library facilities, especially for the public, under both civic and parochial auspices; and Evelyn was one of those responsible for the plan of a public library for every parish. A final outcome of Evelyn's work with Naudé was in his own library, where his choice, arrangement, and catalogue were very much in accord with Naudé's principles. His more than four thousand books were classified under six main headings and more than a hundred subheadings, and the whole is carefully listed in Evelyn's catalogue of 1687. The only major point of departure by Evelyn was the pleasure he took in fancy bindings, some of which he designed and even made himself.

Evelyn's last literary production of 1661, the most prolific year of his life, was a satiric essay on men's fashions, *Tyrannus, or the Mode; in a Discourse of the Sumptuary Laws.* While it made no great splash at the time, it is the sort of social record which grows in value and interest, as its continual reprintings attest.[5] After a brief preface somewhat ponderously forecasts the frivolous mood of this "impertinencie" (as he calls his light essays), Evelyn moves briskly into the body of the work. He has three topics to discuss: propriety of dress and the symbolic relationship between clothes and their wearers, the English subservience to French designers and the frequent alterations of dress, and the nature of some appropriate male garments and the means which might insure their adoption.

For Evelyn, propriety in dress for a man means stability and manliness. He makes the first point positively: "inconstancies, which however allowable in the weaker, becomes not the viriler Sex" (II, 330). The second point he effects by ridicule: "Behold we one of our Silken Camelions and aery Gallants, making his addresses to his Mistress, and you would sometimes think yourself in the country of the Amazons" (II, 330). Also, that rank should be designated by dress seems a truism to Evelyn, and he complains, "How many times have I saluted the fine Man for the Master, and stood with my hat off to the gay Feather, when I found the Bird to be all this while but a Daw" (II, 328). He points out that Plato allowed only courtesans and comedians to change their style of dress "since 'twas but a kind of hippocrisie to be every day in a new shape and *Mascarad*" (II, 327).

He grants that clothes do not make the man, jocularly acknowledging, "I would not judge of the *Monk* by the Hood he wears" (II, 323). But he is equally convinced that people are impressed by the dignity or uniqueness of an outfit, illustrating this conviction with the opinion that "the *Swisse* had not been now a Nation, but for keeping to their prodigious Breeches" (II, 323). The ultimate to which he carries the psychological relationship of man and his dress is found in the statement that "those who seldom change the *Mode* of their country, have as seldom alter'd their *affections* to the Prince" (II, 326). The idea is a variation on one which had currency in the Renaissance, particularly in courtesy books, that a nation lacking a national costume lacked independence and loyalty.

It is hard to know which Evelyn deplored more, the transience of French fashion, the ludicrousness of it, or French dictation in this field. Fanciful invention gives vividness to his descriptions of changing styles. At one time clothes are vastly loose and at another "sew'd up in sacks, . . . Now we are all Twist, & at a distance look like a pair of Tongs, and anon stuff'd out behind like a *Dutchman*" (II, 324–25). He has heard that "as unstable as a *Christian's Hat*" has become a Turkish expression of execration (II, 331). A touch of the Jonsonian epigrammatic style is found in this portrait: "It was a fine silken thing which I spied walking th' other day through *Westminster Hall,* that had as much Ribbon about him as would have plundered six shops . . . all his body was drest like a May-pole or a *Tom o' Bedlams* Cap. A Fregat newly rigg'd kept not half such a clatter in a storme, as this Puppets Streamers did when the Wind was in his Shrouds" (II, 325). He assures us that a French designer claimed to have invented French fashions never worn in France to satisfy the insatiable English. Repeatedly, he berates his countrymen for following the French lead: "why should I dance after a Monsieur's Flajolet only, that have a set of *English* viols for my concert?" (II, 327). "*Mode* is a Tyrant" (II, 331) is his summation at the end of the essay, and it explains both his title and his aversion.

Evelyn's recommendations blend something of moderation with his idea of naturalness: "I am neither fond of the round hoofe, nor of the long shooes, but for that which best fits my foot" (II, 330). He describes the mean by exaggerating the extremes: certain coats require "a Shooinghorn" to put them on; pleated pantaloons "are a kind of Hermaphrodite" and make a man look as if he "were supported with a pair of *Ionic* Pillars" (II, 330); extremely short skirts are fit only for the character with eyes and mouth in the shoulders and breast who appears in Sir John Mandeville's fabulous tales of his travels. Evelyn gives particular attention to neckwear: the band which was then in fashion and the cravat which was coming in. He deplores the stiffness, like "pastboard," of "that piece of Wainscot which supports it [the band] about our necks" (II, 331). For indoor wear, he favors "the stately and easy Vest," a full-length, loose-fitting, cassocklike garment. The cravat and the vest were among the fashions that were later adopted in England, possibly thanks to *Tyrannus.* But Evelyn's other recommendations were ignored; Charles continued to be a fashion follower rather than leader, and no sumptuary laws were passed.

While Evelyn is distinctly original and imaginative in this work, a body of similar material contributed to his handling of the topic. Biblical and Classical comments on dress play a large part. Contemporary prose satiric essays have some influence. Evelyn's treatment of genteel attitudes toward clothes echoes courtesy books. The same good humor found in character writing in portraits of gallants or courtiers informs Evelyn's ridicule. Another probable influence is the verse satirists—John Marston, John Hall,

Ben Jonson—who were sharper than Evelyn but whose works served as models for his witty similes, epigrams, and aphorisms.

What is good about *Tyrannus,* besides the play of wit and the consistent good humor of the piece, is that the precise reference to contemporary fashion do not, with a very few exceptions, make for obscurity. Considering that the express purpose of the work was immediate reform, this fact is the more remarkable. As a vivid portrait of the Restoration beau, *Tyrannus* complements the comedies of the day in which speech and action figure more than description.

IV   *The History of Trades and* Sculptura

The most productive year of Evelyn's literary career was 1661, with two original books and a pamphlet, two reportorial essays, and a lengthy translation. In contrast, 1662 was very quiet, with but one publication, a book that derived from a meeting of the Royal Society: on January 16, 1661, Evelyn recorded in his diary that he had presented "to the *Philosophic Club* . . . my Circle of *Mechanical* Trades." Deriving partly from Francis Bacon, this was an ambitious plan to survey comprehensively the histories of the various important trades and crafts. The design—as grandiose as his projected *Elysium Britannicum,* which in fact would have been comprehended in the master outline—was beyond one man's power, as Evelyn himself acknowledged in a letter to Robert Boyle (Aug. 9, 1659). He finished parts and occasionally referred to the general plan thereafter, but it never became, it seems, the central motivation of his literary career that he may have originally hoped for and that some scholars have claimed it to be.[6]

His immediate contribution to the plan was undertaken at the recommendation of the Royal Society, *Sculptura: or the History and Art of Chalcography and Engraving in Copper,* presented to the Society on June 10, 1662. In a leisurely dedication to the scientist Robert Boyle, a fellow member of the Royal Society, Evelyn expressed the wish "to employ the whole remainder of the life which God shall assigne me . . . cultivating the sciences, and advancing . . . useful knowledge, emancipated from the strong contentions and little fruit of the former; envy, and imposture of the latter ages" (*Misc. Writ.,* 245). The extensive prefatory material includes also a list of the almost one hundred authors consulted for the work. The text itself consists of six chapters: the nature of sculpture; its origins; its progress in biblical and Classical times; the invention and the practitioners of chalcography, drawing, and design; and the new engraving technique of mezzotint.

Sculptura has little to offer the student of literature. Evelyn's continuing endeavor to develop a prose style fitted to scientific exposition is evident, but he shows less grace here than elsewhere. There is an amusing, because remarkably naïve, account of the evolution of art from "the protoplast of our father Adam" onward (263). Evelyn is briefly entertaining on the subject of inn signs, arguing in colorful and heated fashion against the proliferation of pictures of royalty made by "vile and wretched bunglers" and hung "for signes, among cats and owles, dogs and asses, at the pleasure of every tavern and tippling-house" (271). A passage in Chapter 5 on the educational uses of art for young people is interesting. But for the general reader the bright spots are few.

Even for the student of art history, the usefulness of *Sculptura* is limited. Attempting to treat sculpture and engraving in one history is not very meaningful. The arrangement of the material is unsatisfactory; the facts are ill-digested and sometimes in error; and many of the early English engravers are not mentioned at all. Part of the problem was the scarcity of precedent. Much of the material was based on Evelyn's firsthand observations.

Two further charges against the book have nothing to do with its being a pioneer work: one, that Evelyn is wrong about the originator of mezzotints; second, that he fails to describe that process. While some scholars have suspected Evelyn of deliberate deception in attributing the invention to Charles II's cousin Prince Rupert, most regard his error as disingenuous; at any rate, he did correct it in Chapter 8 of a later work, *Numismata*. His omission of a description of the process is peculiar. He says that he leaves it "aenigmatical"; Horace Walpole scornfully wrote, "he checked his bounty, and determined not to prostitute the arcanum, but to disclose it only to the elect. . . . They would be reckoned mountebanks in this age, who should pretend to instruct, without informing; and one cannot help wondering that so beneficent a nature as Mr. Evelyn's should juggle with mankind." [7] Whatever the cause of his change of heart, Evelyn did shortly thereafter give the facts into the hands of the Royal Society.

In spite of its faults, the book has held some lasting interest. It is the first history of engraving in England and was a serious scientific contribution for its day. It carried the first public announcement of the invention of the mezzotint and originally contained a sample mezzotint print done from a plate made by Prince Rupert; extant copies including this engraving are prized today. For all these reasons, for its facts, and for its record of contemporary taste, it has been reprinted several times and is still consulted by print collectors and art historians.

Besides recording the past, the book made some direct impressions on art and art literature. Evelyn exaggerated in his claim that his account of the mezzotint "set so many artists on Worke, that they soone arived to that perfection it is since come, emulating the tenderest miniature" (Mar. 13, 1661). But art historians credit Evelyn with arousing interest in the process. His laudation, in *Sculptura,* of landscapes as a subject for art played its part in their rapidly increasing popularity. His encouragement of print collecting started others, such as Samuel Pepys and Elias Ashmole, forming fine private collections. His application to art criticism of the standards and context of the philosophy of science was formative in a significant, if short-lived, trend. And most far-reaching in the subsequent evolution of art history was Evelyn's approach of addressing himself primarily to viewers rather than to artists, of teaching taste more than practice.

V   *Verses to Tuke*

Far less ambitious than the *Sculptura* but a good bit more amusing was Evelyn's next composition, one occasioned by the fact that his cousin by marriage Samuel Tuke had written a play. While it is questionable whether Evelyn was ever really keen about playgoing, he attended a variety of theatrical entertainments with some regularity in the first years after the reopening of the London theaters. Eventually his disgust with the lewdity and "atheisticall liberty, fowle & undecent" of the stage put him off (Oct. 18, 1666); but he was not yet out of patience in January, 1663, when Tuke's *The Adventures of Five Hours* was produced. Evelyn attended a rehearsal and a regular performance of the play; and he joined Abraham Cowley among others in writing commendatory verses.[8]

Evelyn's contribution, entitled "Upon my Worthy Kinsman Colonel *Tuke*, His Incomparable Play," consists of fourteen pentameter couplets ostensibly in praise of Tuke but, in fact, curiously ambiguous. The verses start with the powerful but confusing exhortation: "I Would you had not Writ! but 'tis too late." This presumably mock-disappointment is explained thus: in his first attempt at the drama, Tuke has reached perfection: "Your Head has brush'd the Sphears," Evelyn exclaims, and then tops this hyperbole with "You in Five Hours have here performed more,/Than in Five Ages all our Bards before." The problem, consequently, is that there is nowhere, further, for Tuke to go— as "The Fates do Limits to each thing dispense."

In conventional doubletalk, Evelyn both treats the play as original (it was a very Anglicized and moralized adaptation of a Spanish work) and also asserts that Tuke can surpass himself only by writing a play of his own. In a vivid couplet, he refers to adverse criticism, or perhaps resentment, which has been directed at Tuke; but he dismisses it lightly: "What though the Serpent bite, and Fools revile,/He breaks his Teeth who thinks to hurt your File." In fact, the play, immensely popular, had an extraordinarily long run and numerous reprintings. Evelyn alludes to these facts, implying that Tuke has put all competitors out of business. Yet, Evelyn notes, Tuke has sworn he will not write another play. On the strength of that avowal, the verses end on much the same note as they began, with a command that the theater, run by William Davenant, be closed: "Sir *William* shut your Door."

All of this verse is obviously meant to be a gracefully jesting compliment. But the curious esthetic theory that sets such limits "To Poets rage" and the crisp satisfaction with which Evelyn greets Tuke's oath not to write again betray the fact that Evelyn really had little love for the stage, even at its most moral. This underlying tension makes the verses more interesting than eulogistic work generally is. Cowley's contribution, which follows Evelyn's, is more mellifluous and smoothly unified; but Evelyn's brisk and strange humor is distinctly fresh.

VI Sylva; *Freart*

By now, Evelyn's books had established such a reputation for
him that he could be sure of a favorable reception for anything
he chose to write. His greatest triumph was still to come, *Sylva,
or a Discourse of Forest-Trees.*

Once again, the subject was chosen for Evelyn. The occasion
was a lumber shortage. The civil wars, increased tillage of the
soil, industrial use of wood as fuel, and recent losses of ships in
battle had depleted supplies so alarmingly that the navy called
on the Royal Society for solutions. Evelyn with a committee developed a detailed program of reforestation, one based on his
personal experiences on estates, his extensive observations of gardens and plantations, and his wide reading from the ancients
through the most recent authorities. His proposal to the Royal Society was that the landed gentry should be the ones to undertake
extensive plantings: they had the patriotism and the means; a
book could supply the one thing they gravely lacked—the necessary technical information. The Royal Society directed Evelyn
to prepare the book; and, with his usual intense industry, he took
only about six months to gather his materials, compose his text,
and prepare it for the press. It was published in February, 1664.

The first edition of *Sylva* consists of three rather independent
works bound in the one volume: *Sylva* itself, a treatise on cider,
and a gardener's almanac. Each work has its own dedication,
preface, and table of contents. The themes are related, but there
is no organic unity for the whole, and the styles of the three differ as suits their form.

A preface "To the Reader" explains the purpose and occasion
of *Sylva*. The tone is heavy-handedly jocose, calling the title page
the *"Porch* of this *Wooden Edifice"* and hoping that "these dry
sticks" will provide the reader with "any *Sap."* Similarly incon-
gruous for a modern reader is Evelyn's choice of authorities—
Edmund Waller, Tasso, and Xerxes—to prove the urgency of the
contemporary situation. The text itself is methodical and comprehensive. Taking each tree in turn, it examines in detail how,
where, and when to plant, prune, and fell each kind, and what
the industrial, nutritional, and domestic uses of each are. The
last quarter of the book gives more general principles and statistics, aphorisms, laws, and statutes about trees.

The next part of the volume—*Pomona, or an Appendix Concerning Fruit-Trees, in relation to Cider. The making and several ways of ordering it*—is about trees, too, but for cider-making rather than for lumbering. The dedication and preface explain that the purpose of the book is to profit the state and the public health by encouraging the English to produce and drink cider instead of beer or wine. Two arguments against beer are that hops are destructive of gound timber, tending to infect it with diseases and even devour it, and they are "rather a *Medical*, than *Alimental* Vegetable." Evelyn is dismayed to behold a "Nation, which now takes a *Potion* for a refreshment, and drinks its very *Bread-corn!*" By contrast, cider is a beverage which will "chase away that unsociable *Spleen*." That wine offers no real competition is established by an anecdote and a barrage of words, as Evelyn expresses the wish that those who prefer wine might see "but the *Cheat* themselves; the *Sophistications, Transformations, Transmutations, Adulterations, Bastardizings, Brewings, Trickings*, and *Compassings* of this Sophisticated God they adore." Evelyn's exposition of the cultivation of fruit trees is a brief affair; it is followed by a collection of other people's recipes, discourses, sets of aphorisms, and other chitchat on cider.

Last in the volume comes *Kalendarium Hortense: or, the Gard-'ners Almanac; Directing what He is to do Monethly, throughout the Year.* After a brief introduction and, in some copies a brief dedication to Abraham Cowley, Evelyn tells month by month what is to be done in the orchard and in the kitchen garden, in the parterre and the flower garden, as well as what fruits are in prime and what flowers. He concludes with essays on greenhouses and lists of fruit trees. Eminently practical, the *Kalendarium* proved to be one of Evelyn's most popular works: besides its inclusion each time *Sylva* was reprinted, this almanac was issued separately almost a dozen times during Evelyn's lifetime. Today, it is a relatively rare book, for the copies have simply been worn out through use.

Voluminous as was this first edition of *Sylva*—it consists of more than two hundred pages, folio—it was only the beginning for Evelyn. He had not so much written a book as started a career. For the rest of his life, he sought further information, corrected and enlarged the text, and issued new editions. In 1706, when his final revision was published, there had already been

some two dozen editions in all, counting the separate editions of
the parts as well as the collected work. Although a detailed account of the revisions in each of these three works is not really
needed, a few particulars indicate the trends. Evelyn records the
success of the first edition in the new dedication to the king,
Sylva 1670:

This Second Edition of *Sylva,* after more than a *Thousand Copies* had
been Bought up, and dispers'd of the *First Impression* in much lesse
time than two *Years* space (which *Book-sellers* assure us is a very
extraordinary thing in *Volumes* of this bulk), comes now again to pay
its *Homage* to your Serene *Majesty,* . . . [and] to acquaint *You,* that
it has been the *sole* Occasion of furnishing your almost exhausted
Dominions, with more (I dare say) than *two Millions* of *Timber-Trees;*
besides infinite *Others,* which have been Propagated within the *three
Nations,* at the *Instigation,* and by the *Direction* of this *Work.*

Undoubtedly a degree of hyperbole is involved in this claim, but
it is based on a large measure of truth. The address to the reader
is embellished with several more puns, exhorting the young head
of a family to give thought to sylvan, as well as to human, husbandry and propagation. There are additional commendatory
prefaces, including a dozen Greek verses by John Evelyn, Jr., then
fourteen. An index of nineteen double-columned pages is characterized, as are all Evelyn's indexes, by the heterogeneity of the
entries: for example, "Arke," "Chaucer," "Dotards"; and such
sequences as "Lopping, Lotus, Love, Lucus, Lungs, Luxury," and
"Policy, Politicians, Polling, Polishing, Poor, Pores, Pots, Poultry,
Powder, Prayer, Presages"—all part of reforestation.

Besides these additions, many chapters in *Sylva* are greatly enlarged and three new ones aded, the most significant of which is
a highly rhetorical "Historical Account of the Sacrednesse, and
Use of standing Groves &c." containing much esoteric lore on
religious beliefs, superstitions, and practices associated with forests. Among the other items in this new edition, the most significant alteration is the expansion of the dedication to Cowley. It
describes his rural life as ideal, filled with leisure, liberty, books,
meditations, and friends; "Who would not, like *You, Cacher sa
vie?*" Evelyn asks him (3). In all, the second edition contains over
three hundred pages.

In his royal dedication to the 1679 edition, Evelyn made his
claims for the effects of *Sylva* even stronger: "many *Millions* of

Timber-Trees (besides infinite *others*) have been *Propagated* . . . by the sole *Direction* of this *Work*." Likewise, the preface to the reader is revised to answer those who wonder what contributions have been made by the Royal Society. To some who have asked insolently, Evelyn replies: "It is not therefore to gratifie these *magnificent Fops*, whose *Talents* reach but to the adjusting of their *Peruques*, courting a *Miss*, or at the farthest writing a smutty, or scurrilous *Libel* (which they would have to pass for genuine Wit)." To sincere inquirers, Evelyn answers that the society, judging as "*Ruinous* and *Crazy*" the system of knowledge before its time, has endeavored "by pulling down the decay'd and sinking wall to erect a *better*." This work has been done by "almost innumerable . . . *Tryals*, and *Experiments* through the large, and ample field both of Art and Nature." Specific accomplishments, published works, inquiries from abroad, correspondence— all bear witness to this aim.

An "Advertisement" to this 1679 edition notes that, while *Sylva* is not designed "for the sake of our Ordinary *Rustics*, but for the more *Ingenious* . . . Persons of *Quality*," Evelyn would not have his unfamiliar vocabulary be a "*prejudice* to the *meaner capacities*." So he appends a glossary of about fifty terms, with such entries as "*Ablaqueation*, laying bare the *Roots*; . . . *Compost*, Dung; . . . *Heterogeneous*, repugnant; *Homogeneous*, agreeable; *Hyemation*, protection in *Winter*; *Ichnographie*, Ground-plot."

New to this volume is an essay by Cowley acknowledging Evelyn's flattering dedication of *Kalendarium Hortense*. In a prose introduction and then in eleven stanzas of poetry, Cowley echoes Evelyn's rural enthusiasm and agrees that gardening is his favorite pastime: "you choose this for your Wife, though you have hundreds of other Arts for your Concubines." [9] With further amplifications of its text and the inclusion of several other treatises by Evelyn and a poem on gardens translated from the French by his son John, the third edition of *Sylva* roughly totals five hundred pages.

In the year of Evelyn's death, 1706, with the spelling of its title changed to *Silva*, the fourth edition was issued, including some but not all of Evelyn's alterations. This *Silva* contains Cowley's "The Garden"; *Silva*; Evelyn's son's translation of Book II of Rapin's *Of Gardens*; *Terra*; *Pomona*; *Acetaria*; the *Kalendarium Hortense*; and all the prefaces and appendixes. Almost seven hundred pages long, it became the basis for subsequent editions.

From 1664 on, *Sylva* was considered to be the apex of Evelyn's achievement. When Pepys prevailed on Evelyn to have his portrait done for Pepys's library, this book shared the limelight: "I sat for my Picture to Mr. *Kneller,* . . . holding my *Sylva* in my right hand." Evelyn was—disinterestedly—pleased as his diary entry indicates: "nor did Kneller ever paint better & more masterly work" (July 8, 1689). The book was an unexpectedly large moneymaker, and Evelyn regretted that he had let the printers get the profit instead of having assigned it to the Royal Society. Royal favor toward Evelyn was promoted by *Sylva,* including appointment on the Council of Foreign Plantations "with a salarie of 500 pounds per Annum to encourage me"—but not as inspector of Royal Forests, for which "I confesse I had an inclination" (Letter to Lady Sunderland, Aug. 4, 1690). Samuel Butler, among other satirists, honored him with satiric lines, making fun of his ". . . several new-found remedies,/Of curing wounds and scabs in trees." [10]

As for its literary merit, most readers have treated this as an incidental feature; and with this attitude, they find much to praise. Sir Walter Scott, for example, in *Kenilworth* (Chap. 12) called *Sylva* "the manual of British planters" and Evelyn's *Memoirs* "the manual of English gentlemen." Both are uniquely eminent, in his opinion, but his phrasing says nothing specific about literary merit. A century later, the book is commended in a survey of those later seventeenth-century works which attempted to give new literary expression to science: "the genius of the man was such that the resulting book, instead of being a dull report, is yet alive with the pleasure of the writer . . . a bulletin has been made a piece of literature." [11] Evelyn's biographers have spoken of the wealth of information in *Sylva,* Evelyn's competence and ardor, his orderly method, and his controlled artistry of phrasing. All these commentators evaluate *Sylva* strictly within the context of scientific literature.

Those critics who have approached the work as a piece of literature have had less favorable comments to make, since *Sylva* unquestionably falls short of its inherent possibilities.[12] A detailed analysis of his style has the value of showing what Evelyn himself was attempting, where his criteria and sensibilities fit into the development of this type of writing, and precisely what are his merits and failures.

First of all, one must distinguish the highly utilitarian, "tumultuary Method," as he himself called the style of *Pomona* and of *Kalendarium Hortense*,[13] in which factual brevity in almost outline fashion is the keynote, from the leisurely, humanistic *Sylva*. In the preface to *Pomona*, Evelyn gives a rather detailed commentary on his style. Declaring that *Pomona* was "not intended for a queint or elaborate piece of *Art*," Evelyn continues, "nor is it the design of the *Royal Society* to accumulate *Repetitions* when they can be avoided." Hence, Evelyn has produced a sketchy work, "such rude, and imperfect *Draughts* being far better in their esteem (and according to my Lord *Bacon's*) than such as are adorn'd with more *Pomp*, and ostentous *Circumstances*, for a pretence to *Perfection*" (62). There is almost an opposition established in this statement between functional and esthetic values. This streamlined style, awkward as it may be at times in Evelyn's hands, is the progenitor of modern expository writing; and, as such, it may well be considered extraliterary.

But in *Sylva*, Evelyn fashioned his prose with great deliberation, evidently aiming at other goals than sheer functionality. Chief among these is his attempt to choose his diction and rhetoric to embody the mood and voice which are of the essence of the work. Toward the end of the work, he speaks self-consciously of this effect: "if . . . in this Rustick *Discourse* [I have] us'd the freedom of a plain *Forester;* it is the *Person* I was commanded to *put on*" (323). The words "plain Forester" are conventionally modest; the point of importance is that he has deliberately assumed a given voice. The characteristics of this voice are authority, reasonableness, maturity, and near-devotion to the subject. What makes these qualities not only tolerable but pleasing and convincing for many readers is the careful use of stylistic elements, particularly these: direct address, homely anecdote, understatement, authoritative imperatives, and exclamatory debunking.

Where Evelyn is in command of his subject, he speaks with finality; where he is not, he makes no pretense. For instance, listing beverages to be made from birch and other trees, he concludes: "And I have seen a *Composition* of an admirable *sudorific*, and *diuretic* for all Affections of the *Liver*, out of the *like* of the

Elm, which might yet be drunk daily as our *Coffee* is, and with no less delight; But *Quacking* is not my *Trade"* (98). When he indulges his fancy, he maintains an air of irony: *"Diana's* presidency in *Silvis* was not so much celebrated to credit the *Fictions* of the *Poets,* as for the Dominion of that moist *Planet,* and her influence over *Timber:* . . . For my part, I am not so much inclin'd to these *Criticisms,* that I should altogether govern a *Felling* at the pleasure of this mutable *Lady"* (240).

Even stronger language is used to set aside superstitious lore: "I am astonish'd at the Universal Confidence of some [earlier editions said "all our Botanists"], that a *Serpent* will rather creep into the *Fire,* than over a twig of *Ash;* this is an old *Imposture* of *Pliny's,* who either took it up upon trust, or we mistake the *Tree"* (62). Yet immediately adjacent to this skepticism is the following report, a late addition in the evolving *Silva:* "But (whether by the Power of *Magick* or *Nature,* I determine not) I have heard it affirm'd with great Confidence and upon Experience, That the *Rupture* to which many *Children* are obnoxious, is Healed, by passing the *Infant* thro' a wide Cleft made in the *Bole* or Stem of a growing *Ash-Tree* . . . that the Cleft of the Tree suffer'd to *close* and *coalesce,* as it will, the *Rupture* of the Child, being carefully bound up, will not only abate, but be perfectly cur'd" (62).

Amusing as these curiosities about ash trees may be, Evelyn knows what is more and what is less important and uses hyperbole at times but understatement more often. He opens the chapter on ash trees with the dramatic claim that a man he knew produced an ash grove worth fifty thousand pounds: "These are pretty Encouragements, for a small and pleasant Industry" (58).

Evelyn freely personifies trees and anthropomorphizes their behavior—not sentimentally since their importance is always seen in terms of their utility for men—but in a fashion which both vitalizes the trees and makes the challenge to the forester seem the more dynamic. He speaks of "obstinate, and deep rooting," opposes early pruning for the ash with the phrase "Cut not his *Head,"* advises that pruning at the proper time "will cause him to shoot prodigiously," and states that "the best *Ash* delights in the best Land" (59–60).

The "Historical Account of the Sacrednesse, and Use of standing Groves, &c," added in 1670, is far more elaborate in style than the other chapters. An immense number of texts and recollections provide Evelyn with endless illustrations of his subject and with strange and fascinating customs and details. But, presumably to show respect for the subject and partly to give shape to such a wealth of material, Evelyn employs many inversions, periodic constructions, lengthy sequences of parallel structures, and much difficult and allusive vocabulary. There is no question that the effect lacks the rhythms and persuasion of Thomas Browne, whose style it suggests; but Evelyn's rhetoric has its moments, as in his description of gardens as places for prayer and sepulture and in his attack on "our late prodigious *Spoilers*" (the Commonwealth men).

Sylva is not in the front rank of baroque prose because it is only incidentally baroque in its techniques. It is a first-rate example of seventeenth-century scientific literature, and it has tremendous significance in the history of ideas and of sensibilities. Stephen Switzer in 1718 stated its importance in terms that are old-fashioned to twentieth-century ears but that identify with astonishing perspective the special value of *Sylva*. Switzer, who called Evelyn "one of the greatest Writers we have had in Gardening, as well as in several other Matters," said that "This Ingenious and learned Person, like another *Virgil*, was appointed for the Retrieving the Calamities of *England*, and reanimating the Spirit of his Country-men, for their Planting and Sowing of Woods." His eminently quotable conclusion is that to Evelyn "it is owing that Gard'ning can speak proper *English*." [14] Evelyn's forerunners treated nature in one of two ways: for some, the facts of nature were so extraliterary that questions of style never arose; for the others, nature was a book, a set of symbols, an allegory to be read into for more ultimate meanings and, therefore, style mattered very much for these, but nature in itself relatively little. Evelyn, by contrast, cherished natural phenomena for themselves and devoted to them his best stylistic efforts. This way of combining nature and art—soon to become so common—was just emerging in Evelyn's time; and *Sylva* is a landmark in its literary development.

In a letter to Lady Sunderland of August 4, 1690, Evelyn relates his publishing activities of the year 1664. After speaking about *Sylva*, the letter continues: "taking notice of our want of bookes of architecture in the English tongue, I published those

most useful directions of Ten of the best Authors on that subject
... all of them written in French, Latine, or Italian, & so not intelligible to our mechanics." The work to which he refers is a
translation from the French of *A Parallel of the Antient Architecture with the Modern* by Roland Freart, Sieur de Chambray.
That Evelyn conceived this work to be a companion piece to
Sylva becomes clear as we continue reading his letter to Lady
Sunderland: "In this method I thought properly to begin with
planting trees, because they would require time for growth and
be advancing to delight & shade at least ... while building might
be raised and finish'd in a sum'r or two if the owner pleas'd."

Like the *Sylva*, although not on quite so grand a scale, *A Parallel* was to go through many editions, involving extensive revision
and amplification by Evelyn. The work consists of several dedications by both Evelyn and Freart; the text of Freart's *A Parallel*,
copiously illustrated with engraved plates; a lengthy original essay by Evelyn entitled "An Account of Architects and Architecture"; and another translation, a "Treatise of Statues" by Leon
Baptista Alberti. Later editions carried new prefatory material as
well as Sir Henry Wotton's *The Elements of Architecture*. The
first edition was dedicated to Charles II, whom Evelyn calls "so
Royal a Builder," for having rebuilt in three to four years more
than had been destroyed in twenty, or more than had been built
in one hundred.[15]

A preface follows that is addressed to the "Superintendent and
Surveyor of his Majestie's Building and Works," John Denham
in 1664 and to Christopher Wren when Evelyn rewrote it in
1680. In the preface Evelyn says that, while he is publishing
Freart's work at the command of the Royal Society, he has had
the topic in hand for over ten years. Associating environment and
temperament, as he did in *Fumifugium,* he comments: "It is from
the *assymmetry* of our *Buildings,* want of decorum and proportion in our *Houses,* that the irregularity of our *humours* and affections may be shrewdly discern'd." He then, in the preface of
1664, provides a highly descriptive, if not too relevant, picture of
the London streets, improvement of which he strongly recommends, for "the saving of *Wheels* and *Carriages,* the cure of
noysom *Gutters,* the *deobstruction* of *Encounters* . . . and the
preserving of both the *Mother* and the *Babe;* so many of the *fair-
Sex* and their *Off-Spring* having *perish'd* by *mischances* (as I am

credibly inform'd) from the ruggedness of the unequal *Streets*."
The text analyzes and describes the principal Greek and Roman orders of architectural design. There is a line-engraved illus-
tration for each chapter, "the best printed & designd," according
to the king, "that he had seene" (Diary, Oct. 28, 1664); and the
plates are indeed of splendid quality. The buildings Freart used to
exemplify the various principles were largely known to Evelyn
from his Continental travels; and, while Freart did not neglect
modern architectural developments, his preference was with the
old styles. Evelyn felt at home with the material and in entire
sympathy with Freart's point of view.

Evelyn's preface to "An Account of Architects and Architecture" explains that this essay augments an incomplete portion of
Freart's work, the explanation of "a few of the hard words, technical terms belonging to the art, the etymologies whereof he
thought necessary to interpret" (*Misc. Writ.*, 353). This section
is not a glossary but a detailed analysis. He starts with the archi-
tect, for whom he demands a training, a responsibility, and an
extensive authority practically unheard of in English practice before that time. Next he explores the general terms of architecture
and then the particular and concrete ones.

His exposition illustrates his points, but otherwise it is without
rhetorical flourishes except for one passage, an outburst against
Gothic architecture. This style he describes as "a certain fan-
tastical and licencious manner of building, which we have since
call'd *Modern* (or *Gothic* rather), congestions of heavy, dark,
melancholy, and monkish piles, . . . full of fret and lamentable
imagery" (365). He despises the "slender and misquine pillars";
the "trite and busy carvings"; and all the "sharp angles, jetties,
narrow lights, lame statues, lace and other cutwork and crinkle
crankle" (366). He lists the outstanding Gothic cathedrals at
home and abroad, "besides the innumberal monasteries and
gloomy cells" (267). Against these he sets the classically inspired marvels of his own century. Critics have ridiculed Evelyn's
blindness to the beauties of Gothic art, but they acknowledge
in the same breath that English building was in dire need of re-
vitalizing at the time of Evelyn's writing and that apparently
French taste was the only immediate inspiration. But, whatever
today's opinion of Evelyn's taste be, his work became the standard
textbook for several generations of English builders.[16]

In literary style, *A Parallel* has little interest. Not solely for the gentry as was *Sylva*, *A Parallel* addresses a mixed audience—the builders themselves, some of whom are educated and some not. Evelyn even apologizes for what erudition he does supply: "nor let any man imagine we do at all obscure this design by adorning it with now and then a refin'd and philological research; since, whilst I seek to gratify the politer students of this magnificent art, I am not in least disdainful of the lowest condescentions to the capacities of the most vulgar understandings" (353). An additional consequence of this difference in audience is that Evelyn makes no attempt to adorn his style, generally speaking, in either the translation or in the original parts of *A Parallel*. Aside from the impassioned attack on Gothicism, the tone, vocabulary, and method are baldly factual, and the style is distinguished only by the rather sprawling sentence structure.

The Royal Society gave Evelyn one last assignment for this year, the translation of a French tract on religion, and the publication carries the date 1664 on its title page. It was not actually released until the next year and shortly after was followed by a sequel; consequently, it fits more naturally with the next group of Evelyn's works. Even without this final task, these three years saw a staggering quantity of work by Evelyn, most of it commissioned but all of it genuinely interesting to him and growing out of his own pursuits. The variety is perhaps not quite so great as in his first period of publication, but it is still impressive: geography; politics; civic improvement; current events; library science; fashions in clothes, sculpture, and engraving; theatrical criticism; reforestation; gardening; and architecture. In genre and style, too, his works display remarkable versatility, as one finds encomiastic, descriptive, reportorial, anecdotal, satiric, and simple expository prose, the highly ornamental style of *Sylva*, and the commendatory verses. Also, the period produced two works of superlative rank for Evelyn's popularity: the *Sylva* which throughout his life was considered his best work and the *Fumifugium* which has been the most reprinted of his books (aside from his diary) in the twentieth century. Evelyn's writing career was not one third over by the end of 1664, but never again would he have three such successful years as these.

CHAPTER 3

1665-1685—Editorial and Personal Preoccupations

THREE changes mark Evelyn's literary activities after 1665. He slowed his pace sharply, rarely producing more than one book or essay a year and none at all in some years. Although he continued to do assignments for the Royal Society, he was far more inclined to choose his own topics and to devote himself to writings not necessarily intended for publication. And he spent much time revising and reissuing past works, new editions of which were his only publications in many a year.

I Other Men's Ideas

The translation which Evelyn published in the winter of 1665 was the first of two attacks on the Jesuits and on papal infallibility. Fears of Catholicism had increased greatly since the Restoration, and the rumor persisted that Charles was secretly a Catholic. The Royal Society and the king felt that the works of two French Catholic theologians, Antoine Arnauld and Pierre Nicole, both in varying degrees pro-Jansenist and anti-Jesuit, would be valuable publications because of the English situation. A recent English translation of Pascal's *Lettres Provinciales* was called *The Mysterie of Jesuitism;* so Evelyn called his collection of letters and essays *Another Part of the Mystery of Jesuitism, Together with The Imaginary Heresy.* Part of Evelyn always felt the unity of Christianity far more strongly than the divisive elements. The only original part of the volume, Evelyn's dedication, deplores not Catholicism but "that a *Church* which pretends so much to Puritie . . . should suffer such swarms of impure *Insects* among themselves."

Evelyn published the translation anonymously; for, as he wrote to Robert Boyle, "So little credit there is in these days in doing any thing for the interest of religion" (Nov. 23, 1664). Credit came from the king, however: "This night being at *White hall,* his Majestie came to me standing in the Withdrawing roome, & gave me thanks for publishing the *Mysterie* of *Jesuitisme,* which he said he had carried 2 days in his pocket, read it, & encouragd me, at which I did not a little wonder" (Jan. 26, 1665). Not only was there royal approbation, but also an order to do a sequel. Scarcely a month after the publication of the first translation, Evelyn wrote thus to the Lord Chancellor: "Being late come home, imagine me turning over y^r close printed memoires, and shrinking up my shoulders; yet wth a resolution of surmounting the difficulty . . . I am perfectly dispos'd to serve, even in the greatest of drudgeries, the translation of bookes. But why call I this a drudgery? who would not be proud of the service? By the slight tast of it, I find God & the King concerned, . . . nor is it small in my esteeme that God directs you to make use of me in any thing which relates to ye Church, though in my secular station" (Feb. 9, 1665). Rarely did Evelyn write so frankly to men of such high position.

This next translation is *The Pernicious Consequences of the New Heresie of the Jesuites against the King and the State,* written by Pierre Nicole in 1664 and presented by Evelyn to the king on March 1, 1666. Nicole's attack on the "new heresy" is based on his claim that "the power to depose *Kings* is a necessary consequent of *Infallibility*" (23). Evelyn's Dedicatory Preface harps on this same threat for page after page, listing papal tyrannies and various victims of church persecution, until he has worked himself up into a near-panic: "My hand trembles to proceed to the rest." But proceed he does, with terrible allegations against past popes, especially in respect to English royalty, and with a solemn warning to "our own incomparable PRINCE." Evelyn's utter sincerity, his genuine dread that "the Doctrine of Obedience to the Civil Magistrate" will be once again overthrown, and also his utter dedication to the Church of England give power to this preface. His passion produces the rhythms of a speech more than of written prose, and the shorter sentences and more pointed parallelism have an effectiveness lacking in many of his other works. The translation may have been drudgery, but the topic was not all that uncongenial.

Between these two translations, Evelyn published several works. Besides the *Narrative of the Encounter between the*

French and Spanish Embassadours, written in 1661 but issued formally now for the first time, there were two short, original scientific essays. In one, the "Snowpits in Italy," Evelyn presents in unadorned prose the location, size, and method of preparation of the pits in which snow (beaten into ice) was stored in the winter for use in other seasons. Robert Boyle, the editor of *History of Cold* in which Evelyn's essay appears, introduces the material thus: "I shall not injure so justly esteem'd a stile as his, to deliver his description in any other words, than those ensuing ones, wherein I received it from him." [1] Further evidence of admiration for Evelyn's utilitarian prose style appears in the sketch of him in the *Biographia Britannia,* where "Snowpits in Italy" is spoken of as "an admirable specimen of that care with which he registered his discoveries, as well as the curiosity which prompted him to enquire into every thing worthy of notice, either natural or artificial, in the countries through which he passed." [2] The contents of the other essay are made fairly clear from the lengthy title: "An Advertisement of a way of making more lively counterfaits of Nature in wax, then are extant in Painting: And of a new kinde of Maps in a low relievo. Both practiced in France." This two-page exposition was presented to the Royal Society and published in their *Philosophical Transactions* (Nov. 6, 1665).

With *The English Vineyard Vindicated* of 1666, Evelyn was back in his native habitat, the garden. In this book, he did for grapes and wine what in *Pomona* he had done for apples or pears and cider; and the work had something of the same success, first on its own and then often reprinted with *The French Gardiner.* The *English Vineyard Vindicated* is not exactly original, for Evelyn issued it as being "by John Rose, Gardener to His Majesty." In a short preface by "Philocepos," he says that the content of this book is entirely Rose's; the pseudonymous author contributed "only its form, and the putting of his Conceptions together, which I have dressed up in as rural a garb as I thought might best become, and recommend them for Practice." [3] At the end of the preface, Evelyn deplores the neglect by the English of grapevines—like trees, he adds; "but of this I have else-where given an account more at large." Then, in case the pseudonym had not been penetrated, "The Vine-Lover" put "*Sylva*" in the margin.

The style of the text is generally clear and direct. Evelyn gives reasons for almost every step; and this method, together with an unusually frequent use of the first person, gives an air of firm authority. Simple as the style is, the voice is that of Evelyn, as when speaking of brambles and their affinity for chalky soil, he adds, "most confident I am, (nor do I speak it upon conjecture only) that there is no Plant whatsoever so conatural to the Vine for soil and situation as this repent, and humble shrub" (16).

II *"Londinum Redivivum"*; Publick Employment

During this summer of 1666, besides working on gardening books (a second edition of *Kalendarium Hortense* appeared in August), Evelyn was asked for a second time to be part of a city-planning commission: the first had studied London streets (1662), and this one was to investigate restoration of the decaying St. Paul's Cathedral. Less than a week after the St. Paul's commission was established, it became abruptly superannuated: "September 2: This fatal night about ten, began that deplorable fire, neere Fishstrette in Lond." For over a week the fire raged, until Evelyn wrote, on September 10, "I went againe to the ruines, for it was no longer a Citty" (Diary, 1666).

It is little wonder that Evelyn was one of those who bestirred themselves immediately to plan for restoration. The fire was still smoldering when, Evelyn wrote, "I presented his Majestie with a Survey of the ruines, and a Plot for a new Citty, with a discourse on it, whereupon, after dinner his Majestie sent for me into the Queenes Bed-chamber, her Majestie & the Duke onely present, where they examind each particular, & discoursd upon them for neere a full houre, seeming to be extreamly pleasd with what I had so early thought on" (Diary, Sept. 13, 1666).

Evelyn's project, called by him "Londinum Redivivum, or London Restored not to its prestine, but to far greater Beauty Commodiousness and magnificence," consisted of an actual proposal for the layout of streets and buildings and a brief essay describing how the plan might be effected.[4] After beginning the essay with how to make use of the rubble, Evelyn recommends widening the infamous Holborn-Fleet channel "not only to be preserv'd sweet . . . but commodious for the intercourse of considerable vessels" (468). He also urges that the streets be wider—thirty feet for the narrowest and one hundred for the principal thoroughfares—and be enlarged at intervals "into piazzas at competant distances" where markets could be held. The location of St.

Paul's should remain the same; but, in general, churches should be fewer, be regularly disposed, and be so located "as to be conspicuous to several streets, as some of the Roman obeliscs are" (468).

For each parish there should be shops, ministers' houses, schools, and a library. He proposes locations and adornment for guild halls, the exchange, warehouses on the waterfront, and five main traverse streets and their intersections. As in *Fumifugium*, he requests the removal of the smoke-producing and otherwise unsavory industries, graveyards, and prisons. He calls for substantial buildings and shops, handsome gates and entries, paved streets as in Rome, enclosed drain spouts from roofs, and a clean system of water pipes. If these advices are ignored, he concludes, "it may possibly become a new indeed, but a very ougly city, when all is done" (470).

None of the many plans proposed for rebuilding the city was accepted, and just how practicable any of them was is a matter of scholarly argument. But Evelyn's has remarkable distinctions; for, more so than any others, it largely preserved the locations of the main thoroughfares, buildings, and water pipes. The vistas it proposed were unknown in England and, in fact, almost anywhere except Rome. His plan would have greatly reduced fire and health hazards. In the months that followed, the streets were slightly widened, drainage and building materials were improved, markets were better located, and Wren was able to build some fifty churches which vastly adorned the city—infinitesimal gains in contrast to the ideal advice of Evelyn and the rest.

Only in the twentieth century has *London Revived* been published as a separate work, with a careful introduction pointing out its sources, characteristics, and merits.[5] So much of Evelyn's proposal incorporates the best developments of city planning since his day and, at the same time, evokes so much of the flavor of old London that the effect is almost poignant. Could 66,000 homeless people have been kept out of 400 ruined streets, while the equivalent of 13,200 houses were being rebuilt, the phoenix might have turned from fable into reality. Evelyn's essay captures a glorious if impractical breadth of vision.

One might think that Evelyn's ineffectuality in these city-planning operations would have dimmed his enthusiasm for working for the common good. But when an anonymous Scots publication appeared in 1666, "A Moral Essay preferring Solitude to Publick Employment and all it's Appanages; such as Fame, Command, Riches, Pleasure, Conversation, etc.," he at once prepared a reply, *Publick Employment and an Active Life Prefer'd to Solitude,* published in February, 1667. The work was an immediate, though short-lived success.

At first reading, one is struck with the faults of the piece, particularly the lack of organization, rather than with its reasons for success. In the preface to the reader, Evelyn describes his essay as "the effects of a very few hours, a cursory pen" (*Misc. Writ.,* 507). Perhaps this haste accounts for his procedure of simply refuting his opponent's points without either adverting clearly to any order in the original essay or imposing one of his own. A further confusion arises from the fact that he does not cite the title of the essay or the author's name (Sir George Mackenzie, which he apparently did not know at the time), referring to Mackenzie simply by the personal pronoun without any antecedent. The effect of some of Evelyn's blows is markedly reduced when the reader is lost in the ambiguous syntax. Recognizing these shortcomings and looking at the essay more as random notes preparatory to composition, one is struck—as so often with Evelyn—by the fertility of ideas; for the number and variety of arguments and illustrations are almost overwhelming.

In defense of the public and active life, Evelyn discusses man's nature, the outcomes of public life, and some analogies. Men's talents complement each other and all are necessary: the meditative life could not exist if there were no active life. Defending ambition as an important element in the active life, Evelyn calls it a good in itself, for it is one of the traits which distinguish men from animals and it becomes a vice only when it is abused. Evelyn asserts that the results of the public and active life also confirm its merits, and he lists the numerous great men whose works have been beneficent and who have remained in public life when they did not have to do so. He claims that public men have been the authors of by far the most notable books; their good example, by being publicly on view, has been efficacious; and their conquests have been the foundation of civilization (although Evelyn must admit that he deplores war). Arguments from analogy set forth the active nature of God, of Christ in the major portion of his life, and of the human organism itself, with the circulatory system seen as microcosmic by Evelyn.

As against these virtues of the active life, Evelyn presents the evils of the solitary life. Since the solitary man cannot pursue his way of life without the active man, since it is unnatural to be alone, and since living for oneself is demonstrably unsatisfactory, the solitary life is evidently by nature not good. Equally, its results are bad—sloth, temptations, and peculiar vices, of which miserliness is but one of the more mentionable—while its proposed good results are often not so; for the occupations of the retired man are many times very silly, his much-acclaimed writing is more often trivia or pedantry than wisdom, and his withdrawal and simplicity of life produce notoriety rather than inconspicuousness.

But the great weight of arguments that Evelyn musters for his side does not prevent him from acknowledging the complexity of the issue: personalities differ; both ways of life can be abused; good and bad examples can be ranged on both sides; and every active man must have some rest, recreation, and meditative solitary time to restore his strength. Moderation in all things is the watchword. As he argues, Evelyn cites abundant authorities to support the arguments. Many of these references he evidently recollected from past readings, but he also reviewed particular passages for this rebuttal. Lactantius, Cicero, Plutarch, Aristotle, Seneca, Suidas, Aelian, Virgil, many books of the Old and New Testaments, Plato, Epicurus, Isocrates are quoted, translated, or paraphrased.

Evelyn's tone in *Publick Employment* is generally intense and direct, but in some passages he employs satire, ridicule, and irony. Denying the "admirable simplicity pretended" for country life, he asks if there is not "overreaching in the purchase of a cow, or a score of sheep? as much contention about the encrochment of a dirty fence? . . . How many oaths and execrations are spent to put off a diseas'd horse? . . . and even greater pride, deadly feud, railing, and traducing, amongst the she-Pharisees, or little things of the neighbourhood, for the upmost place in the church pew?" (*Misc. Writ.*, 524–25). Mackenzie saw King David as a good man led astray by public life; Evelyn responds, "Let it be remembered that he was alone upon the battlements of his palace, and then all the water in Bathsheba's fountain was not cold enough to extinguish his desires" (530).

Evelyn exalts the public life with hyperbolic, pietistic sketches of personified virtues, as in a seventeenth-century frontispiece or as on a commemorative coin; his satire of the inactive life is more in the style of Hieronymus Bosch and Pieter Brueghel, with extraordinary anticipations of William Hogarth, Jean Antoine Watteau, and the pre-Raphaelites: "represent to yourself . . . his country-gentleman taking tobacco, and sleeping after a gorgeous meal; there walks a contemplator, like a ghost in a church-yard, or sits poring on a book whiles his family starves; here lies a gallant at the feet of his pretty female, sighing and looking babies in her eyes . . . on yonder rock an anchorite at his beads; there one picking daisies, another playing at pushpin . . . here one drinks poyson, another hangs himself" (551–52). The caricature is perhaps not entirely in harmony with the rest of the essay, but the exuberance and touch of humor are welcome.

A question which the essay raises is how sincere, or even serious, Evelyn is. In a letter to Cowley, Evelyn says of the essay, "I neither was nor could be serious" (Mar. 12, 1667). In the one personal passage in the book, he claims, "There is no man alive that affects a country life more than my self" (543). He preferred his country residences to London quarters, and entries in his diary often praise rustic and solitary scenes. The question is of some biographical interest, but it is not central to the literary value of the work. For the essay, rather than being a statement of personal commitment or even preference, is an academic discussion or an intellectual exercise. From the medieval debates, through the exercises of the schools, well into the seventeenth century, literature repeatedly displays this taste for exploring both sides of an issue in a formal debating fashion, often with little or no intellectual commitment, but a great display of virtuosity. Evelyn's essay fits with this taste and style.

His ideas, while not especially original, are an interesting compendium of the various arguments which in the late seventeenth century and throughout the eighteenth century were constantly restated in a wide variety of literary forms. Evelyn covers just about all the different forms of active life—that of a prince, a member of the court, a public servant, a philanthropist, or the man of politics, of ideas, or of the arts—and also the degrees of solitude from the eccentric hermit Simon Stylites on his pillar to the highly convivial *"beatus vir"* on Horace's epode. Somewhat deficient in clarity, the work is rich in ideas and vitality.

III   The History of Three Late Famous Impostors; *Other Reporting*

In 1668 Evelyn published his last translation undertaken on assignment, and he expressed in the epistle "To the reader" his distaste for the task. The Royal Society had asked that a committee do for painting what had been done for architecture in *A Parallel of the Ancient Architecture with the Modern;* so Evelyn translated another of Freart's works, *An Idea of the Perfection of Painting.* Freart presents in it the rules which all painters should follow if they would become great and then examines in great detail several famous paintings (especially da Vinci's *Last Supper*), analyzing them in terms of these rules and the axioms on perspective. In the prefatory epistle, Evelyn calls the reader's attention especially to Freart's discussion of decorum; and he himself gives many examples of works by great masters marred by the introduction of inappropriate costume, other types of anachronism, and elements from everyday life too low for the overall subject. He takes exception to Freart's wholesale criticism of Michelangelo but agrees with him in stressing the importance of perspective. Evelyn finds modern painters and architects generally better than their predecessors because they are "learned men, good historians, and generally skill'd in the best antiquities" (*Misc. Writ.,* 561).

Interesting for the event it commemorates is Evelyn's succinct but eloquent dedication "To the Illustrious Henry Howard of Norfolk, Heir-Apparent to that Dukedom." The occasion for praise is that Norfolk, at Evelyn's suggestion, gave to Oxford University the family's collection of glorious Greek statues. These —known as the Arundelian marbles, from the title of the dukedom—were being sadly neglected in the family's London house and garden. Evelyn proposed the gift, arranged the offer, had the statuary catalogued, and received along with Norfolk enthusiastic thanks from Oxford.

An Idea of the Perfection of Painting was important enough at the time, but it is too restricted in its viewpoint to have the lasting appeal of the earlier Freart. It was published just once.

The History of Three Late Famous Impostors of 1669 is a compilation of materials, reported to or read by Evelyn, that have to
do with hoaxes undertaken by or against the Turks. The first two
stories he got from a Western-educated Persian, Pietro Cisii, who
years earlier had exposed the first of these impostors, Padre Otto-
mano. In London in 1668 Cisii discovered another would-be impostor, Mahomed Bei, and revealed the falsity of that man's
claims. Evelyn tells in his diary of having had "much discourse
with Signor *Pietro Cisij* a *Persian* Gent: about the affaires of
Turky to my infinite satisfaction" (Sept. 29, 1668). The third account, about Sabatai Sevi, a self-styled messiah of the Jews, is by
an English diplomat, Sir Paul Rycaut, who in his *History of the
Turkish Empire from the Year 1623 to the Year 1677* (1680) gives
this same report, word for word as in Evelyn, and claims it as
his own.[6]

These three tales are the body of the book, but there are the
usual addenda. In the address to the reader, one finds a brief
account of a fourth impostor's adventures brought abruptly to a
close "in a tipling-house on the rode, where, un-mindful of his
past and character, he call'd for a pot of ale in too good English" (*Misc. Writ.*, 568). After the last tale Evelyn presents "The
History of the Late Final Extirpation and Exilement of the Jewes
out of the Empire of Persia," a legendary explanation that the
Jews were exiled because they gave a false prophecy of the messiah's coming.

The narrative style and skill of the three histories vary greatly.
The first, a sketchy affair overburdened with proper names, tells
of a slave child, captured by the Maltese, who is palmed off as
the son of the Grand Signior but ends up a Dominican priest. It
is an essentially ironic revelation of duplicity in which the Near
East and the West are well matched. The second, Mahomed
Bei's life story, is equally brief but less selective, being a loosely
strung chronicle of his adventures, climaxed simply by the revelation of his true identity as a renegade from Walachia. Witty expressions rather than plotted organization give what literary interest there is to this material.

The third account, by far the longest, concentrates on the cru-
cial year in Sabatai Sevi's life, 1666, when he claimed to be the
messiah, abetted by the rogue Nathan, denominated his prophet.
The Christian world, remembering uneasily the implications of

the number 666 in the Book of the Apocalypse, had worked itself into a superstitious state in anticipation of this year and the opening paragraphs relate this frame of mind to Sevi's hoax. The extravagance of Sevi's claims and his conniving, the credulity of both the Jews and the Mohammedans, and the bizarre comportment of all concerned produce a comic-opera effect.

Nonliterary considerations may easily preoccupy the reader of *The History of Three Late Impostors,* for Evelyn himself stressed his aim of warning against deception. Because the stories are so strange, one might dismiss them as just one more manifestation of Evelyn's abiding interest in the curious. Or the absurdities could blind one to all other values, although these seem sufficiently deliberate to be amusing. But even if one does not agree that the work has some artistry, it still deserves attention because of its place in the evolution of two literary phenomena: the literary hoax and the Oriental tale.

Not itself a literary hoax of course, *The History of Three Late Famous Impostors* is part of the background of this form. While many of the eighteenth-century literary hoaxers are well known—especially Daniel Defoe, Jonathan Swift (in the Bickerstaffe-Partridge sequence), James Macpherson, and Thomas Chatterton—the larger phenomenon of impostors is less familiar; but they were unusually prevalent in the late seventeenth century and throughout the eighteenth century.[7] In the face of the ever-increasing emphasis on reason and science, a kind of stubborn romantic credulity, eager for exotic and fantastic events and tales, created an irresistible atmosphere for the impostor. Exposure came from those who relentlessly sought to destroy all idols, superstitions, and rosy dreams, who in fact would not tolerate even admitted fictional stories, calling them lies. *The History of Three Late Famous Impostors* is interesting as a very early example of the awareness of both of these attitudes: the yearning for fantasy and for bizarre human behavior, the rejection of illusion.

As for the other phenomenon, the Oriental tale, Evelyn's work is not just a forerunner but a pioneer example which has been neglected by historians of this genre. These scholars speak of the Oriental tale as having sources in the seventeenth century but as not emerging as a well-characterized genre until the early eighteenth century, when the first French and English translations of the *Arabian Nights* provided the model in 1704 and 1705. However, all three of Evelyn's stories contain the essential notes of the Oriental tale: the setting and characters are Near Eastern, the predominant atmosphere is exotic and fantastic, adventure is enjoyed for its own sake, characterization is of the slightest, and the very simple plot lines culminate in the lesson. As the genre developed, it promoted more everyday moral lessons than Evelyn's warning against elaborate impostures, and it was almost always fictional. But, in publishing Cisii's and Rycaut's tales, Evelyn showed once more a sensibility in advance of his times. His work had a continuing popularity, and the form itself flourished for over a hundred years.

The next year saw the publication of two pieces done by Evelyn for the Royal Society. The first is a very brief commendatory letter (dated February 10, 1668) which appeared as an introduction to John Smith's *England's Improvement Reviv'd: in a Treatise of all Manner of Husbandry and Trade* (1670). Smith begins and ends with a discussion of England's trade, claim to the seas, and international relations; the body of the book treats of planting forests of different sizes from one to one thousand acres. Evelyn's letter modestly notes why he was chosen to report on Smith's book: "I have myself been engaged on the same Argument," and he mentions the forthcoming second edition of *Sylva*. Calling Smith's work "industriously perform'd," he concludes "[I] chearfully give it my Approbation." He promises to "Publish a due Encomium" of Smith—but he speaks perfunctorily. Other projects, other interests, and perhaps a feeling that the Royal Society was making too many demands were dimming the extravagance of Evelyn's panegyric prose.

The other publication of 1670, also in the form of a letter, describes a recently invented Spanish agricultural implement that simultaneously plowed, sowed, and harrowed. In February, Evelyn presented his description and the plow to the Royal Society, who published the letter in its *Philosophical Transactions*, June 20, 1670 (*Misc. Writ.*, 621–22).

IV   *The History of the Dutch War and* Navigation and Commerce

Between 1667 and 1674 Evelyn's only original compositions were the two minor contributions just described. Supervising reprintings and new editions of earlier works occupied much of his

time; for over a dozen such publications came out between 1668
and 1680. But the main reason for the seeming decrease in his
writings was a grandiose project begun in 1669 and never completed. Unlike his *Elysium Britannicum* (which, significantly,
was dropped around 1669) and the history of trades, both of
which were his own plans and of central interest to him, this
abortive work—a history of the Dutch War—was imposed upon
him and then abruptly terminated by command.

Very indirectly Evelyn initiated the venture, for in a letter to
the treasurer he made the proposal that, as there was no royal
historiographer at the moment, one of his relatives might be ad-
vantageously used to prepare a reply to certain accusations in
connection with the recent Dutch War (to Thomas Clifford, Feb.
1, 1669). With some alacrity, the king altered the authorship and
the scope; and, addressing himself to Evelyn, "he began to tempt
me about writing the Dutch-Warr &c." (Diary, Feb. 13, 1669).
Evelyn procrastinated, for he wanted no part of the job himself.
But he knew a command when he heard one. For five years he
gathered materials, original documents wherever possible, studied
and organized these, and started the writing. Meanwhile, the war
resumed. On January 9, 1674, he records in his diary: "Sent for
next morning to *Lond:* by his Majestie to write some thing against
the *Hollanders,* about the Duty of the flag & fisherie: so returned
with some papers." These papers were published in May, 1674,
with the title *Navigation and Commerce, Their Original and
Progress.* But the timing was amiss, for by now peace had been
restored. Evelyn recorded the fate of the publication and its relation to his history of the Dutch War:

his Majestie told me, he must recall it formaly, but gave order that
what Copies should be publiquely seiz'd to pacifie the Ambassador
should immediately be restord to the Printer, & that neither he nor
the *Vendor* should be molested: The truth is, that which touch'd the
Hollander, was much lesse, than what the *King himselfe* furnish'd
me with, & oblig'd me to publish, having caus'd it to be read to him
'ere it went to the presse. . . . The noise of this books suppression,
made it be presently bought up, & turn'd much to the Stationer['s]
advantage: Nor was it other, than the meere preface, prepard to be
praefix'd to my Historie of the whole *Warr;* which I now pursu'd no
farther. (Aug. 19, 1674)

Taken as a "prefix," *Navigation and Commerce* is a lengthy

affair—over a hundred pages in its original printing. In view, however, of its full title—"Containing a Succinct Account of Traffick in General; its Benefits and Improvements: of Discoveries, Wars, and Conflicts at Sea, from the original of Navigation to this Day; with Special Regard to the English Nation; Their Several Voyages and Expeditions, to the Beginning of our late Differences with Holland; in which His Majesties Title to the Dominion of the Sea is Asserted, against the Novel, and later Pretenders"—the book is almost epigrammatic. Evelyn considers the wise lay-out of the seas; the early competition in navigation; the origins and connection between commerce, empire, and building of ships; the period of explorations and discovery—Columbus and the English heroes, Drake especially. Then he switches from historical survey to the main part of his assignment, "His Majesties Title to the Dominion of the Sea." He makes a case for England's priority in the northern seas and for its past kindnesses to Holland, and he establishes England's right in a quick glimpse from creation through the Romans, Anglo-Saxons, and Normans to more documented times. The conclusion is that denial of the English claims of sovereignty at sea is simple insolence.

The work purports to be utterly rational, dispassionate, and logical. Evelyn strengthens this pose of simple reasonableness by intermixing with recondite facts disarming avowals of ignorance or conjecture: "We shall not adventure to divine who the hardy person was who first resolv'd to trust himself to a plank, within an inch of death, to compel the woods to descend into the waters, and to back the most impetuous and unconstant element; though probably, and for many reasons, some-body long before the deluge" (*Misc. Writ.*, 636). Then he tells the reader that Pyrrhon the Lydian was the one who first bent planks by fire, that Hippus the Tyrian was responsible for "carricks and onerary vessels of prodigious bulk" (637), and that there were ships equipped with fruit gardens and shade trees.

Evelyn's sense of wonder vividly recreates the transient pageant of the seas: "The famous Brundusium (whence the great Pompey fled from the fortune of Caesar) is now quite choak'd-up. ... But what's become of hundreds we might name; Spina near Ravenna, Luna in Etruria, Lesbos, and even Athens her self? ... The stately Genoa (which once employ'd twice-twenty thousand hands in the silken manufacture) is now, with her-elder-sister

Venice, ebbing apace; Venice, I say, the belov'd of the sea, seems now forlorne" (650).

With less documentation than spirit, he recounts the story of "that fortunate stranger Columbus, prompted by a magnanimous genius and a little philosophy" (654), and he debates rival claims for the discovery of America without diminishing the glory of Columbus. He calls Drake "this demi-god," "that inestimable jewel" (656 and 658); and so infectious is his enthusiasm over the exploits of the discoverers that one may momentarily overlook his chauvinism: "these brave persons, scorning any longer to creep by shoars, and be oblig'd to uncertain constellations, plow'd-up unfathomable abysses, without ken of earth or heaven, and really accomplish'd actions beyond all that the poets of old, or any former record, fruitful in wonders, could invent or relate" (656).

Though Evelyn wrote with verve, there can be no question but that this assignment was immensely distasteful to him. He found the research nearly overwhelming, stressing in a letter to Clifford "how im'ence an ocean I have pass'd to bring it home to the argument in hand, and yet in how contracted a space I have assembl'd together that multitude of particulars the most illustrious" (Aug. 31, 1671). He resented the cloud under which *Navigation and Commerce* was distributed and the lack of thanks for his work.

Far more distressing to Evelyn than the waste of time and lack of gratitude, however, was the fact that he compromised his conscience in this work in a most untypical fashion. He confesses this fact in great detail in a letter to Pepys, showing that he had sifted the evidence to find proofs of England's maritime claims, had in fact failed to find them, but had written as if the data were established—"by which you may conclude how suspicious wise men should be of other histories and historians too, how confident & specious soever, unlesse it were almost demonstration, that the authors had no interest of their owne to serve, & were not influenc'd by their superiors, or the publiq cry" (Sept. 19, 1682). His confession is joined with exhortations that Pepys pursue to completion a history of the navy on which he had worked for some thirty years and for which Evelyn sent him all his manuscripts on the Dutch War. Hopefully, Pepys was to set straight what Evelyn had equivocated. But this is the end of the story—for references to the manuscripts diminish and presumably the papers were eventually destroyed.

Navigation and Commerce has the typical faults and merits of seventeenth-century history. First of all, it undertakes vastly too much; second, it intermingles fact and legend, precise documentation and hearsay; third, it starts with a thesis and fits the facts to it. It hardly deserves the name of history in any modern sense. At its best, Evelyn's presentation contains some insights, an excitement felt from the mere statement of facts, the general sense of wonder and drama, and the vivid record of a political-economic sensibility which is a part of the seventeenth-century milieu.

V   Surrey; Terra; A Devotionairie Book

From history, Evelyn turned to topography, his subject being Surrey, where the Evelyn family estate of Wotton was located. Although, as second son, Evelyn did not come into his own at Wotton until the 1690's, his interest in the county was lifelong.

In 1675, he wrote a letter to John Aubrey, eventually included in Aubrey's *Natural History of Surrey* (1719), giving some random notes on Wotton and its environs. These include some public data and some personal recollections supplementing the information contained in an early draft of Aubrey's work, which Evelyn saw in manuscript. Some are the kind of oddity which constantly fascinated Evelyn: a prodigiously large plank cut from a local oak, and a gigantic skeleton found in the churchyard. Others are little-known facts about the fauna, the makeup of the soil, and local history, with details about Roman relics, former industries, and remarkable kitchen spits. The easy combination of objective fact and personal response that so often characterizes Evelyn's writing is found here as when, having itemized the varieties of stone in certain peripheral pits and adjacent "sugar-loaf mountains," he exclaims that these "with the boscage upon them, and little torrents between, make such a solitude as I have never seen any place more horridly agreeable and romantick" (*Misc. Writ.,* 688).

Twenty years later, when William Camden's *Britannia* was reissued (1695), Evelyn contributed the notes on Surrey; and they are similar to the material furnished to Aubrey. Heterogeneity is still the keynote, with references to a famous Roman way, past prelates of Guildford, the clothier business in bygone days, medicinal wells, and a high lookout spot commanding a panoramic view. There is a mild but pervasive mortuary emphasis, for within so brief an essay he speaks of funerary urns, the custom of planting rose trees on graves, the Wotton churchyard, and the aforementioned gigantic skeleton, which he here specifies as having been over nine feet tall. Again the tone is one of ostensibly dispassionate reporting, but one is aware of Evelyn's customary *élan* in the face of any facts, his enthusiasm slightly augmented here by family pride.

The year before Evelyn sent Aubrey the notes on Surrey, the Royal Society decided that regular presentations of experimental discourses by members would be desirable. Evelyn was an early contributor to this program: "I read my first discourse of *Earth & Vegetation* before the *Royal Society,* as a lecture in Course after Sir Rob: *Southwell* had read his the weeke before on Water: I was commanded to print it by our President & the Suffrage of the *Society*" (Diary, Apr. 29, 1675). The work appeared in 1676 as *A Philosophical Discourse of Earth, Relating to the Culture and Improvement of it for Vegetation, and the Propagation of Plants.* Later the word *Terra* was prefixed and became the generally used short title.

Evelyn's dedication of *Terra* is a conventionally modest disclaimer of the inadequacies of his own work in contrast with that of other members. These protestations are invalidated by the text, for it is a solid mass of pertinent factual information. The discourse is an essay of almost two hundred pages; though not divided into chapters, the material follows an orderly plan, consisting of "What I mean by Earth; . . . the several sorts and kinds of Earth . . . [and] how we may best improve it to the Uses of the Husbandman, the Forester, and the Gardner" (9–10). Evelyn spends some time speculating on such basic concepts as the origins and principles of earth and then moves on to very practical advice on how to prepare and irrigate the earth and fertilize it— with animal, mineral, and vegetable fertilizers. He discusses the variations required for different types of soil and locations of plants. The very mundane practicality of the subject prompts his closing summation: "Thus I have exercis'd Your Lordships and these Gentlemens Patience with a dull Discourse of Earth, Mould and soil" (181).

Rhetorical embellishment plays but a small part in *Terra*, con-

siderably less than in *Sylva* for example. There may have been
some haste in the preparation, and Evelyn may have thought the
earth to be less worthy of ornamental prose than were trees and
forests. But probably too the deliberate efforts within the Royal
Society to evolve a spare, lucid prose style serviceable for exposition found their counterpart in such a work as this one. Evelyn's sentences have still the flavor of seventeenth-century leisure
and gentility; but, aside from strictly functional syntactic patterns
and the usual sprinkling of allusions to classical authorities, his
style is self-effacing. The subject was the thing, and the consequent practical value of the book earned it an enthusiastic reception. In 1678, Evelyn incorporated it into the *Sylva* edition of
that year; thereafter, *Terra* regularly appeared in that volume.

Somewhere in the late 1670's and early 1680's Evelyn put together, in manuscript only, notes on religious thoughts and practices which were the product of at least thirty years' jottings. The
restricted religious situation of pre-Restoration days is reflected
in some of them. The 1662 version of the Church of England
prayer book is the pattern for the order of presentation. During
the 1670's he had shared these notes in some form with his young
spiritual advisee Margaret Godolphin. Finally, he recast them in
the present shape and addressed them to a friend—an unspecified
and probably indeterminate one. Only in the twentieth century
was this material published, as *A Devotionarie Book of John
Evelyn of Wotton, 1620–1706.*[8]

The work is in three sections. The first, "Of Frequent Communion," is a subject on which Evelyn had feelings unusually
strong for his day; for his diary regularly records the occasions of
his communicating and notes his preparations for the sacrament.
In *A Devotionarie Book*, he reviews the scriptural background
of communion, deals with the possible deterrents (scrupulosity,
thoughtless habituation, undue familiarity), and rhapsodizes over
the joys of the practice. "He . . . saved & rescu'd us from eternal
ruine, and being undon for ever," (11) he exclaims, playing elegant variations on titles for the "Banquet of Love" and acknowledging, "You see (my holy Friend) how far I am Transported"
(13).

The second part, "Mental Communion," is about an equally
common activity for Evelyn since, during the Commonwealth,
Church of England services were generally prohibited in public

and at times subject to penalty even when celebrated in private. But, even after religious persecution ended, Evelyn saw a need for formulas for mental communion during times of illness or when other obstacles prevented church attendance. This section contains the commandments, proposed for meditation; pious ejaculations; prayers corresponding to various parts of the communion service; and parts of psalms and similar supplementary prayers. The tone is strongly personal and emotional.

The last half of the book, with the curious title "Entertainements," is composed of sequences of aphorisms designed as subjects for meditations; and these alternate with prayers which are labelled "ejaculations" and are exclamatory in construction but rather lengthier than is common for that form. The materials are, some of them, paraphrases of his readings, some commonplaces, and some of them original; but all are assimilated into a common style.

A Devotionarie Book is a pleasant expression of one phase of seventeenth-century spirituality, for such documents are not all that common from 1640 onward. Yet it represents one very real mode of religious experience of the time and presents it with characteristic grace and charm.

Indeed, part of the value and impact of the work is owing to the style. As usual with aphorisms, parallel structure and antithesis are used to advantage: "To suffer Temtation is a misery; but to set on its Mortification, an occasion of virtue" (48); "Sorrow for sinn, is not Repentance (no, nor Teares) but the absolute leaving it" (49); "He who promises pardon to the penitent, does not promise Repentance to the sinner" (51). Occasionally the contrast is complex to the point of obscurity: "Whatsoever is ineffective of an Holy Life, is not Repentance" (48). So habitual is the use of antithesis that Evelyn's departures from it sometimes fall flat or are confusing. For example, "Jeasting at holy things, is next the material part of the irremissible sinn" (54) might well leave at least the modern reader cold. Elsewhere the unfulfilled antithesis sharpens the attention, simply because of the surprise, as in such maxims as these: "One who had *realy* Repented of the greatest Acts, and habits of Sinn; may comfortably say, He hath a good Conscience" (51); "Be allways ready, for what you allways expect" (56); and "The Best, and almost onely use of Friends & Friendship is the Advantage of Admonishing one another" (59).

The ideas are often at least as interesting as the expression, especially in relation to seventeenth-century thought. "Security is not from Signes but from Duty" (48) is presumably a warning against enthusiasm. The image, in this next, had peculiar immediacy for the mid-century reader: "In our smaller sinns, *Christ* is not presently ejected; but as a Prince oppressed, who still continues his Clayme" (50). Apparently more informative than imperative is this dictum: "Some deliberate Wasting sinns, Committed by Religious persons; thô they Recover: is yet commonly punished with some temporary Judgement" (50). Evelyn rejects the peculiar emphasis on deathbed piety so often found in contemporary spiritual writings, saying "Living well, not dying, is that which (by God's mercy) will save us" (51). But he sounds his own notes of near Puritanism in "A good name, ones Credit, and our Eyes, admitt no Revellery" (56), and in the curious economy of "Sorrow for sinn, then best, when equaling the pleasure we took in sinning" (49). A similarly rigorous emphasis which consorts very oddly with Evelyn's own ruling passion appears in a pair of "entertainments": "Obedience is the voluntary death of the Will, and Life without Curiosity" and "God has given us enough for use, not for Curiosity" (54).

VI *Some Minor Pieces*

In terms of publication, the 1680's were the leanest period in Evelyn's career. He did no translating; and reprints, which had been voluminous in the 1670's and many of which were new editions involving much rewriting, dropped off almost completely. A few brief essays and complimentary prefaces, contributed to journals and other men's books, were his total appearance in print in the years 1681–84.

The first of these was a commendatory letter to a horticulturist writer, who recognized the value of an introduction by Evelyn. Before publication, T. Langford showed Evelyn his *Plain and Full Instructions to raise all sorts of Fruit-Trees that prosper in England.* Evelyn returned a brief but hearty commendation which was printed as one of the prefaces when the book appeared (1681). In Langford's book Evelyn found, he said, "the intire Mystery so very generously discover'd from its very Rudiments, to its full perfection; that . . . I know of nothing extant which exceeds it."

In 1682, Evelyn's one publication was a set of polite verses composed almost forty years before. When Evelyn was in Padua in April, 1646, George Rogers, a young English medical student, received his doctor's degree there. To celebrate this event, several English visitors, including Edmund Waller, honored Rogers with commendatory poems; and Evelyn's contribution is eight lines of youthfully extravagant Latin verse. He credits Oxford with having first formed and perfected Rogers, speaks of the violence and bloodshed in England, and asserts that England will not perish from her wounds since Rogers is now equipped to heal his native land. The imagery is stock—palms, muses, laurel-crowned temples—but the turn of thought is appropriate and graceful. These bygone exercises went to press because Rogers was publishing an oration which he gave in honor of William Harvey at the London College of Medicine in 1681. Filling out the volume were his old graduation address from Padua and the seven poems prompted by it.[9]

Probably some time this same year, a fellow member of the Royal Society who edited a magazine elicited an item from Evelyn. "An Account of Bread . . . Entituled, Panificium, or the several manners of making Bread in France. Where, by universal consent, the best Bread in the World is eaten" appeared in the January 16, 1682 issue of John Houghton's *A Collection of Letters for the Improvement of Husbandry and Trade*. In *The French Gardiner*, Evelyn had refused to treat culinary arts, but here he competently itemizes the various ingredients and their requisite merits, especially the water, and then gives a variety of recipes. In a helter-skelter burst of ideas at the end, he tells how to freshen stale bread and how to use the ferment of cherry wine as yeast, recommends that English housewives be consulted for recipes of English breads, and requests a description of a new kind of oven and ideas on the best ways of brewing beer and ale. All this material is presented with earnest precision and no flourishes.

VII The Life of Mrs. Godolphin

Judging by the correspondence, scholars conclude that it was during these years, 1682–84, that Evelyn composed *The Life of*

Mrs. Godolphin, a strange book but one of his most valued works in terms of his personal life and personality and its genre and peculiar graces. Mrs. Godolphin, born Margaret Blagge, was attached to the court from her youth, but was distinguished for her spiritual interests; and she became a close friend to Evelyn when she was not yet twenty, and he was fifty. They visited each other, prayed and performed works of mercy, and corresponded often (but arranged that their letters not survive them). They made a pact of friendship in 1672, when Evelyn wrote this description of her: "a rare example of so much piety, & Virtue in so greate a Witt, beauty & perfection; This miracle of a young Lady in a licentious Court & so deprav'd an age: She now delivered me the ☆ under her owne hand, & it shall be *Inviolable*" (Diary, Oct. 16, 1672). That pentacle or star-shaped symbol of their friendship long baffled editors of Evelyn's diary, where it often appears without a name as a designation for Margaret. The bond somehow survived her marriage—kept a secret, even from Evelyn, for a year —and periods of separation. Her death in childbirth in 1678 was a great loss to Evelyn.

Evelyn had several reasons for writing her life. The most immediate were that Lady Sylvius, a close friend of Margaret's, asked him to and that preparing this memorial in some measure assuaged his grief. Personal feelings aside, her life invited recording on its own merits; for she was a surprising combination of beauty, charm, talent, genuine virtue, asceticism, prayerfulness, and very practical charity—and she was all these things despite the setting of the elegant and profane Restoration court. A final consideration, undoubtedly, was the reason behind all seventeenth-century spiritual biographies: glorifying God and giving the reader a sound, concrete example of proper behavior toward God, authority, family, and neighbor.

Evelyn's materials were her letters, diary, and recorded spiritual recollections and memoranda, together with his extraordinarily intimate acquaintance with her thoughts as well as with her life and associates. True to the contemporary ideals for biography which favored the inclusion of only what was genuinely significant and uplifting, he was accurately factual but carefully selective both of events and of interpretations. He completed the life around 1685, gave one manuscript to Lady Sylvius and a somewhat different one, years later, to Godolphin; for there was never any thought in his mind of publication. Only in the nineteenth century, when a bishop saw the edifying use to which the material could be put, did it appear in print, whereupon it immediately prospered.[10]

The Life of Mrs. Godolphin is a loosely chronological survey interspersed with the autobiographic documents; each stage is commented upon by Evelyn. He addresses Lady Sylvius throughout—by title, not by name—and thus presumes a wholly sympathetic response from the reader. It concludes with a "Picture," an extended character sketch of Margaret, which is in effect a eulogy. Evelyn's tone is frankly adulatory and his style exclamatory. After the long account of her death, he bursts out "O *unparallel'd Losse! O Griefe Indicible, by me never to be forgotten! never to be O'recome! . . .* THUS, *Began, Lived,* and *Ended* this *Incomparable Christian, Virgin, Wife* & *Friend . . .* But, he were a rare *Artist* indeede, could reach The *Original,* & give those last & *Living Touches,* which should make it *Breath:* But *Madam,* thats not to be Express'd by *Lights* & *Shades,* which is altogether *Illustrious,* and has nothing in it Dark." (79, 83–84). His constant theme is the rarity of Margaret's gifts, her fitness for emulation, and the grievousness of her loss.

The lengthy quotations from Margaret's writings complement his approach; for, while he generalizes and tends to provide emphasis, what he quotes concentrates on the particular and reports it with understatement or a minimally impassioned response. Reading Evelyn's statement "I have frequently heard her say; She loved to be at Funerals, & in the house of Mourning" (13), a modern reader might suspect her of pious phrases or even morbidity and him of fatuousness. But her words on the subject—in a *memento mori* she wrote for herself—are sharply corrective of these impressions; for there one observes specific cases, individualizing details, and totally natural reactions:

A Poore-Woman dead, worn to skin & bones wth a Consumption; she made no Complaints, but trusted in God . . .

My Mother Died, at first Surpriz'd and very unwilling; she was afterwards Resign'd . . .

The D——esse died, a Princesse honourd, in power: had much Wit, much mony, much esteeme: She was full of un-speakable torture, & died (poore Creature!) in Doubt of her Religion, without any Sacrament, or Divine by her, like a poor Wretch: None Remembred her after one

Weeke: None sorry for her: She smelt extreamely; was tost, and flung about, & every one did what they would with that stately Carcasse:—What is this World! What is Greatenesse! (12)

This ejaculation is clearly not a perfunctory, sanctimonious one; it is a spontaneous outcry under the hard shock of life's realities.

Similarly, her lists of resolutions, though aimed at a perfection that may seem impractical, achieve remarkable credibility from the details of precise situations and the implicit acknowledgments of personal frailty. Evelyn stresses Margaret's indifference to dress (18), with no hint that she could ever be difficult with her lady's maid; but she gives us this glimpse into her dressing room: "In Dressing, I must Consider how little it signifys to ye Saving of my Soule, and how foolish it is to be Angry about a thing so impertinent" (14).

Evelyn recounts the general dismay of the court when Margaret's suit to be released from service was finally granted, and she took her leave: "Is Mrs *Blagge* going (says a faire Creature) why stay I here any longer? Others, That the Court had never such a *star* in all its *Hemisphere;* and verily, I had not seen so universal a damp upon the Spirits of every one that knew her" (33). One finds no reason to doubt Evelyn's account, but the scene is given perspective by recalling Margaret's own picture of her behavior and her associates' response: "Now as to pleasure, they are speaking of *Plays,* and Laughing at devout People: Well, I will Laugh at my selfe for my Impertinencys . . . Avoid those people when I come into the Drawing-roome . . . Go not to the *Dutchesse* of *Monmoth,* above once a Weeke, except we dresse to Rehearse"—Margaret was once prevailed on to take part in a court production of a pastoral comedy—"and then Cary a Book with me to read . . . Be sure never to talk to the *King* when they speake filthily, tho' I be Laugh'd at" (16). Margaret had no illusions about her world's reception of her singularity.

What results in the biography is a fourfold picture. This charming young woman emerges as a compound of strong feeling and good common sense. One gets a much less complete but nonetheless forceful impression of the author. An interestingly different view of Restoration court life is provided. And, finally, the book provides a very close look at seventeenth-century spirituality, its introspection; its intense prayer life; and its concentration on sin, repentance, and death, together with the idea that one must relate to the world, perform kindly acts, live and evidence charity.

The reputation of *The Life of Mrs. Godolphin* has varied over the years as the taste and criteria for biography have altered. To the nineteenth-century reader, hers was a saint's life, pure and simple, providing an edifying example of spiritual life, especially suitable for young women. With the twentieth century, the taste in biography turned to human, in preference to spiritual, values; and, by this new criterion, *The Life of Mrs. Godolphin* again found admirers, with particular interest in the concept of friendship that Evelyn sets forth.[11] However, the other new approach in the twentieth century to writing and criticizing biography—the ultrarealistic and debunking attitude—produced fresh appraisals.

In two unsympathetic, almost cynical biographical studies of Evelyn, W. G. Hiscock charged that, while Evelyn pretended disinterested zeal toward Margaret, he was in fact infatuated with her, used their spiritual interests as a hold upon her, tried jealously to prevent her marrying, and wrote an equivocal biography to deceive posterity.[12] Hiscock voiced the modern assumption that absolute altruism is no more likely in a spiritual than in any other close friendship. On the other hand, he failed to find any evidence whatever that the relationship went beyond unexpressed emotional states. The would-be exposé has thus clarified the merits of *The Life of Mrs. Godolphin*. Evelyn did somewhat falsify the image of himself; he did not distort Margaret. And after all, she is the subject. So, even by the severest of twentieth-century criteria for biography, Evelyn's book stands up extraordinarily well.

Considered in relation to other early English biographies, *The Life of Mrs. Godolphin* compares favorably. Like George Cavendish's *Wolsey*, William Roper's *More*, and Fulke Greville's *Sidney*, it strives for an intimate more than a formal public view of its subject. The significant structural features of the book are two: in being addressed to a single person, it is unique among seventeenth-century biographies; it includes letters within the narrative, thus continuing the technique of Izaak Walton and Richard Baxter. Since Evelyn's work was not then published, one cannot attribute to his *Life of Mrs. Godolphin* any direct influence on the genre in its day; but, set alongside its peers, the book is clearly a minor work of art. The genre of saint's life is not for everyone, nor is *The Life of Mrs. Godolphin.* But, for the sensibility to which it is addressed and in terms of its intrinsic intentions, it is successful and has appeal.

VIII *Verses to Creech; the Winter of 1683–84*

During the period of work on *Mrs. Godolphin,* Evelyn's other literary accomplishments were slim. One was occasioned by the publication of the first complete English translation of Lucretius, one prepared by Thomas Creech. Evelyn was one of the contributors of commendatory verses: "To Mr. Creech. On His accurate Version of Lucretius" dwells on the absolute merits of Creech's work, its superiority to Evelyn's translation, and the glories of Lucretius' poem.[13] These ideas are commonplaces, and the technique which distinguishes "To Mr. Creech"—a fine poem and one of Evelyn's best—is the comparison which provides its entire structure. Lucretius' Latin text is seen metaphorically as a new world, as an untapped mine, and as a kind of lush tropical garden. Evelyn is then likened to Columbus as the discoverer, and Creech to Cortez as the one who conquered and brought back the prizes. The metaphor carries the meaning with scarcely any direct statement; for the poem is suave, economical, and rich in its implications. Even such terms as "Hero's," "Demi-God," "glorious Enterprise," and "Crown,"—which would be extravagant applied directly to Creech—have propriety in reference to the explorers. A potentially dry subject is vividly dramatized by the romantic associations of the imagery; the likeness of Keats's "On first looking into Chapman's Homer" is apparent. The lines are a refreshingly alive example of a generally deadly genre. All the qualms of conscience—deep-seated or perfunctory ones, as they may have been—which shook Evelyn when preparing his own translation had apparently been dissipated by the time of Creech's work.

Another piece contemporaneous with *The Life of Mrs. Godolphin* was prompted by the severity of the winter of 1683–84, one of the coldest London had ever experienced: "An Abstract of a Letter from the Worshipful John Evelyn sent to one of the secretaries of the R. Society concerning the dammage done to his gardens by the preceding winter," published in the *Philosophical Transactions* of the Royal Society (April 20, 1684). This piece is typical of Evelyn at his most meticulous; he details the various timber trees, shrubs, fruit trees, and flowers, species by species, and the effects upon each of the prolonged frost. Some fauna come in for attention too, a few fish and a tortoise that died, and the nightingales which survived.

The letter is evidence of his continued esteem for the collecting and reporting of scientific data; and, as such, it fulfills its purpose. That Evelyn was capable of giving a far more lively, picturesque, and stirring account—unsuitable for the Royal Society's needs, but much more appealing to the modern reader—is seen in his diary, particularly in the notes describing the scenes along the Thames. For the river was frozen so solidly that it was "planted with bothes [booths] in formal streetes, as in a Citty, or Continual faire, all sorts of Trades & shops furnished, & full of Commodities, even to a Printing presse, where the People & Ladys tooke a fansy to have their names Printed & the day & yeare set downe, when printed on the *Thames*. . . . Coaches now plied from Westminster to the Temple . . . as in the streetes; also on sleds, sliding with skeetes; . . . it seem'd to be a bacchanalia, Triumph or Carnoval on the Water, whilst it was a severe Judgement upon the Land" (Diary, Jan. 24, 1684).

Three features of Evelyn's life in these years 1665–85 probably account for his having written less copiously: his civic activities in connection with the plague and the Great Fire and as commissioner for sick and wounded seamen and as a member of the Council of Trade and Plantations; the unfulfilled project of the history of the Dutch War; and his friendship with Margaret Godolphin and his sorrow at her death. Even with these preoccupations, the years produced a tally which was creditable for such a gentleman-author. It was now that he wrote his best poem, the commendation of Creech's Lucretius. Several books from this period, while not outstanding, are still pleasing to read: the *London Revived, Publick Employment*, the *Devotionarie Book, Navigation and Commerce*, and *The Life of Mrs. Godolphin*. In relation to literary history, one of his most important works is *The History of Three Late Famous Impostors*.

CHAPTER 4

1686-1706—Fruits of a Lifetime

E VELYN'S last twenty years are remarkable for the continued
liveliness and productiveness of his days. Besides the steady
routine of his private life, there were civic responsibilities, especially two important offices: commissioner for the Privy Seal and
treasurer of Greenwich Hospital. Much more time-consuming
and emotionally draining were the fluctuations of joyful and
tragic events within the family, including the birth of a grandson,
an elopement, several deaths, the marriage of the last surviving
daughter, a gravely distressing legal wrangle over the family estate of Wotton, and finally Evelyn's establishment there as resident and owner. Moreover, the infirmities of advancing age made
all his endeavors more difficult; but, far from reducing his writing
in this period, Evelyn increased it, both his original compositions
and his editorial work. Moreover, he achieved much the same
range of quality as always; for the only mark that his writings
show of his age and of the family crises is his increased preoccupation with topics allied to family interests, but these by no
means engrossed his whole attention. The number and variety of
his publications and completed manuscripts are once again imposing.

I Directions for the Gardiner; The History of Religion

For the benefit of a new gardener apprenticed at Sayes Court
in 1686, Evelyn set to work compiling a one-hundred-page manual of instructions. Although not intended for publication, the
work is broad enough in scope to be serviceable for other gardeners and provides such an agreeable picture of Evelyn and his
garden that it was edited and published in the twentieth century
with Evelyn's own title from the manuscript, *Directions for the
Gardiner at Says-Court. But which may be of use for Other Gardens*.[1]

The book consists of tables, lists, and notes; but none of them is developed at any length (and a few are unfinished). The aim was to be practical in content and in presentation. First, there is a list of the "Termes of Art Used by Learned Gardners." Then almost a third of the book considers each of the plantings on the estate—fruit trees, kitchen garden, physic garden, coronary garden, evergreens, shrubs, forest trees (vulgar and not vulgar), and espaliers—and this section lists their kinds (twenty-one different pears, for example) and explains how they should be arranged. Next are several catalogues, "The Compleat Culture of the Orange . . . after the Holland Way" (49), "Observations for the well-keeping" of various kinds of nurseries and stocks for grafting. More system is restored in the next section, which covers technique: transplanting, watering, pruning, dunging, weeding, hoeing, rolling, and treatment of vermin and diseases. The balance of the book is miscellaneous. The "Directions for Salads" anticipates Evelyn's eventual lengthy study of this subject.

Evelyn's move to Wotton occasions a record of what he had planted there in 1694–96. Several pages headed "Method for the Gardiner" give a weekly and monthly program, starting with the advice to walk about on Monday morning and note what needs doing, dwelling on the rotational mowing and rolling of the lawns, and then epitomizing his own "kalendarium hortense" for the entire year. A table of measures, a list of necessary tools, and an incomplete bee calendar are the last items in the book.

Specialized as the subject is, the book yet has significance for the general reader. As it is addressed at least as much to the squire as to the servant, it can be viewed as a conduct book. Its manner gave status in its own day to gardening as a genteel occupation; moreover, it communicates this view to readers in any age. So concretely does it evoke the atmosphere and charm of seventeenth-century estate living that it is in its own way a minor pastoral idyl, modest though it be in aim and simple in tone.

While there is no sure evidence for dating Evelyn's *History of Religion*, a work not published in his lifetime, the likelihood is that he started it in the 1650's and completed it during this period of his life, especially if the following diary comment is a reference to it: "[Jan.] 22 [1688] . . . This Afternoone I went not to Church, being to finish a Religious Treatise I had undertaken." A voluminous affair, the work filled two fat volumes when it was published—in 1850.[2] Its plan is conventional, for it is both a history and, according to its subtitle, "A Rational Account of the True Religion." Six chapters, the first half of the book, examine the existence and nature of God, of the soul, and then of religion in general. Another three concern Scripture and Jewish practices and sects. Christianity is then approached apologetically, as the fulfillment of Jewish prophecy and as superior to all other religions. Evelyn covers the next sixteen hundred years in about thirty pages. Finally, he notes the "corruptions of the Romish Church"; and he concludes with a strong chapter acclaiming the Church of England.

Preceding the text is the Author's Preface, a leisurely statement of the background, occasion, and purpose of the work. So personal are these elements that the preface amounts to a confession of faith. Little as one might suspect it from his other writings—so that one almost wonders whether this unique statement is more rhetorical than genuinely autobiographic—Evelyn claims to have experienced a religious crisis, in which he "began seriously to consider some time with myself, whether, in truth, all that which had been taught us concerning God, and religion, and honour, and conscience, were not mere chimeras and impostures contrived by our forefathers, crafty men in their generation" (I, xx–xxi). With vivid name calling and fierce denunciation, Evelyn describes the circumstances which created these doubts: the civic suppression and perversion of religion (he evidently means during the Commonwealth), the open sufferance of libertinism, the multiplication of sects, and the new heretical philosophies "deifying the power of matter and the laws of Nature" (I, xxvii) and denying scriptural authority and the immortality and freedom of the soul. The purpose, therefore, of writing *The History of Religion* was to determine for himself whether the traditional teachings were acceptable. The project was a total success: he reached such conviction that "I am not in the least temptation to doubt, much less disbelieve, any one article of our most holy truth" (I, xxxiii).

At the close of the preface, he emphasizes again that he designed the work for his own needs, "never pretending to dress it for the public" (I, xxxiii–xxxiv). Consequently, he has "without any apology, transcribed whole periods out of several authors" (and he lists enough of these by name and by genre to indicate the vast range of his research). He has placed these quotations and paraphrases in his own contexts and often not always troubled himself to "charge the margin with their names." He admits that this practice would be a serious defect had he ever meant to publish the treatise (I, xxxv). And it is typical that, when he put the manuscript in order in the 1680's and wrote the preface—for what purpose he does not say—he still did not trouble himself with tedious annotation.

In contrast to the preface, the text holds no interest for the modern reader with the possible exception of the historian investigating seventeenth-century apologetics. What items are true can be found more readily elsewhere, the truth is mixed with errors, and the so-called proofs are often only firm declarations or citations of authority. The tone is dryly didactic, or dispassionately polemic, with only occasional leavening. On the whole, one is inclined to agree with Evelyn's later description of the book as "a Congestion, hastily put into Chapters . . . full of Errors," [3] with only the preface to draw one to it at all.

Infrequently, Evelyn provides bits of curious lore. For example, he concludes that "pigmies (those diminutive people, or sort of apes or satyrs, so much resembling the little men storied under that name), are, therefore, not of human race, because they have no religion" (I, 261). He tells of parrots that "have been taught to utter, nay, to recite whole psalms, creeds, and litanies" (I, 262). And now and then there are outbursts of enthusiasm. Expatiating on the nature of Christ, Evelyn lists the miracles He performed; at first, Evelyn does so matter-of-factly and then with a crescendo of wonder at their variety and number, culminating in this rhapsody: "Oh, stupendous power! By a word only, without persuasion, He converted an avaricious publican, a wanton Magdalene; the one to leave his usurious bank, the other her sensual pleasure. But so, with one fiat, was the whole universe educed out of nothing; and by a word only were these things effected: He spake, and it was done" (II, 103).

A degree of vitality infuses the lengthy itemizing of heresies, a subject which clearly gave Evelyn consolation. He savors the names and malpractices of the Godescalians, Flagellanti, Fratricelli, *"Framelists,* all of them spawn of the Anabaptists, only changing names. A signal ringleader of this sect was the famous *John of Leyden* and *Kniperdilling,* following out *Nicholas Storke;*

as before were those *Libertines, David George, Quintin,* and
Coppin, who pretended themselves Messiahs" (II, 245)—to say
nothing of "Wicklivians" (who, however, he suspects have been
libeled), Anti-Sabbatarians, and Zuinglium Sacramentarium. As
Evelyn reads the roll call of the heretics, he finds some measure of
sincerity or integrity in a few of them; most he summarily denounces.

II *Editions, Translations, Contributions*

Mundus Muliebris: or, the Ladies Dressing-Room Unlock'd,
published anonymously in 1690, is more an editorial than an original undertaking by Evelyn. He mentions the work in the eulogistic character sketch that he composed for his diary at the
death of Mary, his most accomplished daughter, who died of
smallpox at the age of twenty: "she had read aboundance of
History, & all the best poets, even to Terence, Plautus, Homer,
Vergil, Horace, Ovide, all the best Romances, & modern Poemes,
and could compose very happily, & put in her pretty Symbol, as
in that of the *Mundus Muliebris,* wherein is an enumeration of
the immense variety of the Modes & ornaments belonging to the
Sex" (March 14, 1685).

The preface, Evelyn's own contribution, addresses the work
to a fictitious "young master, who, newly launch'd from the University (where he has lost a year or two) . . . sets up for a *beau*"
(*Misc. Writ.,* 699) but needs to be initiated into the new language and manners of the town. The satiric tone is maintained
while Evelyn briefly ridicules contemporary jargon and pastimes
and then switches to an equally exaggerated picture exalting "the
days of our forefathers (of unhappy memory, simple and plain
men as they were)" (700). This nostalgic and romantic contrast,
though lacking in subtlety, is expressed with very specific details
and evident delight, as Evelyn tells of the time when the "nuptial kirtle, gown, and petticoat, lasted as many anniversaries as
the happy couple liv'd together. . . . They had . . . store of fine
Holland sheets (white as the driven snow). . . . Many things fell
out between the cup and the lip, when happy ale, March beer,
metheglin [a kind of mead], malmesey, and old sherry, got the
ascendant . . . and charity was as warm as the kitchen" (700–701).
The essay is a charming example of primitivistic sentiment.

Mary's text consists of two parts. First, a set of verses—247

lines of octosyllabic couplets with an occasional triplet, called
"A Voyage to Marryland or, The Ladies Dressing-Room"—tells
about the minimal wardrobe of a lady (countless changes of
clothes and accessories) identified in the technical terms of the
day, many of which are French and Italian, and associated with
the activities of the lady's world, the toilet, levee, park, dance,
gambling table, "Nor holy Church is safe, they say" (706, 1.122).
The verse is rough, though not unsuitable to the attitude, which
falls somewhere between Pope's indulgence and Swift's disgust.
Following the poem, the second part is "The Fop-Dictionary, or
An Alphabetical Catalogue of the Hard and Foreign Names and
Terms of the Art Cosmetick, &c. together with Their Interpretations, for Instruction of the Unlearned." The list is an amusing
curiosity because of the words themselves and their subsequent
obsolescence and also because of the definitions which range
from simple translations to whimsical comment:

Surtout. A night-hood covering the entire dress.
Toilet. Corruptly call'd the *twilight*, but originally signifying a little
   cloth.
Tour. An artificial dress of hair on the forehead, &c.
Tres fine. Langage de beau; extremely fine and delicate; *cum multis
   aliis.*
For, besides these, there are a world more; as *assassin,* or *venez a moy,*
   a certain breast-knot, as much as to say, Come to me, Sir, &c: . . .
   (173).

The whole volume is a valuable document in linguistic and
social history and a minor contribution to the growing art of
polite social satire. This genre was to be handled with more grace
in the generation to follow the Evelyns, but it is not unattractively
managed here.[4]
New editions of some of Evelyn's horticultural studies were his
chief literary occupation in 1691. But family pride—and his own
self-esteem—prompted one other diversion, the rewriting of a
sketch of himself for Anthony à Wood's *Athenae Oxoniensis: An
Exact History of all the Writers and Bishops Who have had their
Education in the University of Oxford, from 1500 to 1690.*[5] As an
Oxford alumnus, Evelyn was entitled to a place in this survey.
According to his letter to Wood, May 29, 1691, Evelyn had earlier submitted an account of himself, at Wood's request; and he

now wanted to revise that first draft: "Divers circumstances since that intervening, both as to my fortune (which may possibly transfer my hitherto abode here at Sayes-Court in Kent to the seate of my ancestors in Surry) and an honorable charge, which his late Majestie conferr'd on me, of one of the Commissioners of the Privie Seale." Emphasizing that it is his understanding that the sketch will appear "not as written by me in my owne person (which were a vanitie insuportable)," he further expresses the hope that Wood "would use the sponge, as you thought fit." How much, therefore, of the published entry is by Evelyn one cannot be sure.

The entry, the first under the "Writers of Baliol College," consists of two parts: a five-hundred-word paragraph on the chief events of his life and a list of his writings with brief descriptions. His education, travels abroad, marriage, position in the Royal Society (referred to twice in this short sketch), three public offices, his role in the donation of the Arundelian marbles to Oxford, and his honorary degree are the remembered items. His appointment as a commissioner of the Privy Seal is included. He is described as "an ingenious and polite Person" who "affects a private and studious life," and the passage ends with a quotation from Burnet's *History of the Reformation of the Church of England* describing Evelyn as a man "who is not satisfied to have advanced the knowledge of this Age, by his most useful and successful labours about planting, and divers other ways, but is ready to contribute every thing in his power to perfect other Mens endeavours" (942).

The list of Evelyn's writings includes the most notable through 1684 with the exception of most of the occasional pieces, for both the contributions to other men's works and the more topical of his own separate publications are overlooked. Even *The Character of England* (which was sufficiently enduring to warrant reprinting in 1700), *The State of France, Tyrannus,* and his edition of his daughter's *Mundus Muliebris* receive no mention, but such a relatively insignificant piece as "A Letter . . . concerning the damage done to his Gardens" gets four lines. Although some manuscripts are noted, *Elysium Britannicum* for one, the much more finished *Devotionarie Book, Life of Mrs. Godolphin,* and *History of Religion* are not. Among his translations, no mention is made of the Arnauld and Nicole controversial tracts and of the Le Gendre.

Since this biographic notice is the only one authorized personally by Evelyn, its selection of memorable facts and works is significant—particularly the eminence given his activities relating to the Royal Society; and one can have no doubt that to Evelyn these were his greatest contribution to posterity. The style of the Wood article is less noteworthy than the contents, for it is blithely haphazard, perhaps because of multiple authorship, because of insufficient use of the sponge which Evelyn had recommended, or simply because of a kind of dilettantism on the part of Wood.

The last translation for which Evelyn was responsible was of his own choice and was about one of his favorite topics, *The Compleat Gard'ner*, 1694. The French author, Jean de la Quintinye, a one-time visitor to Sayes Court, had given Evelyn an unpublished "Treatise of Orange-Trees, with the Raising of Melons." This work Evelyn included in *The Compleat Gard'ner*. He also added a preface, an advertisement, some complimentary verses contributed by others, and a dictionary of terms. The English edition filled two volumes, nearly five hundred pages in all. Just how much of the actual translating Evelyn did he made a matter of conjecture by writing in a letter to his brother that "the toil of mere translating would have been very ungrateful," and he indicated that part was done by others.[6] His collaborators were George London and Henry Wise, celebrated royal gardeners who knew both the French language and French gardening and could well have done the work.

The book has no stylistic distinction, attempting nothing more than simple exposition. It has the requisite clarity but little economy. That merit came six years later in 1699 when London and Wise brought out an abridged one-volume version which became the standard edition, with several reprintings in the eighteenth century. None but gardeners did or do read *The Compleat Gard'ner*. It may be categorized an informational handbook and a record of taste but not an artistic creation.

Evelyn's subtitle for the book, *Directions for Cultivating and Right Ordering of Fruit-Gardens, and Kitchen-Gardens*, is a free translation of de la Quintinye's title. His own title, *The Compleat Gard'ner*, has the double merit of brevity (with only slight exaggeration) and of faddishness, as the rage for "compleat" books and journals was still fresh in the seventeenth century. In respect to its topic, the work is "complete," being a compendium of de la Quintinye's vast horticultural knowledge, the product of both study and experimentation. Evelyn's own considerable familiarity with gardens made him respect this thorough and authoritative work.

His equally enthusiastic admiration for London and Wise is the subject of the advertisement, which commends their taste in general and particularly praises Brompton Park, near Kensington, a garden planned by them and notable for the rare plants in its nursery and for the techniques of cultivation employed there. They had learned their ideals—imitation of French gardens and general formality—from the same source as Evelyn, their predecessor as royal gardener, John Rose, the one from whom Evelyn had derived the ideas for *The English Vineyard Vindicated.* A quarter of a century separated that work from *The Compleat Gard'ner* and this was a new generation of gardeners, but Evelyn remained staunchly traditional and Classical and reserved his praise for those who shared his views.

III   *Collecting: Coins and Manuscripts*

Throughout his life, Evelyn was interested in coin collecting. Early in his diary he tells of collections which he viewed in the great houses and museums of the Continent and of coin markets which he attended in the small Italian hill towns where farmers and tourists were gratified by what the plows inadvertently turned up. Just when he decided to write his own *Numismata* is not entirely clear, but his letters suggest that he had it in hand for probably some ten years before it was completed. On New Year's Day, 1698, as he recorded in his diary, "I presented my Booke of Medals &c. to divers noblemen, before I suffered it to be exposed to sale." The engravings were a great success, but the misprints, even with a page-worth of "emendaria" included in the edition, grieved Evelyn greatly.

The full title of the work is *Numismata. A Discourse of Medals Antient and Modern. Together with some Account of Heads and Effigies of Illustrious, and Famous Persons, Sculptures, and Taille-Douce, of Whom we have no Medals Extant; and of the Use to be Derived from them. To which is Added a Digression concerning Physiognomy* (1697). There is a brief dedication, a preface giving a sketch of the history of the work and pointing out the multitude of authors used in its compilation, and an introduction which makes Evelyn's fundamental point: that medals are "the most lasting and (give me leave to call them) Vocal Monuments of Antiquity" (1) in comparison with statues, and manuscripts.

The ten chapters of the text divide the subject in a fairly clear-cut fashion, although neither the logic of the divisions nor their order is overwhelmingly apparent. His first chapters are about the use of medals, medals relating to several nations, and the obverses of medals. Then come the plates and descriptions of ninety-one medals, roughly chronologically arranged, that are mainly Scottish, English, and French. The text resumes with a section on "Other Persons and Things worthy . . . of Medals," which is accompanied by seven more illustrations. The last parts are about inscriptions, how to collect and distinguish true from false mints and how to arrange medals, prints and copperplate engravings, and finally "A Digression concerning Physiognomy." The book concludes with a desultory index in which many of the entries "would puzzle any man to guess how they found their way into a discourse on medals," as Horace Walpole mildly expostulated.[7]

Walpole's remark could apply to large sections of the book, for it is more a catch-all for a lifetime of heterogeneous gleanings than a systematic or comprehensive study. Both the emphasis on the historical lore imprinted on coins and the title "discourse" undoubtedly justified for Evelyn his casual design and his capricious selection. The work has the mark of the truly genteel dilettante, for it is more eighteenth than seventeenth century in its almost total lack of pedantry.

Numismata is a book one can dip into almost at any point with pleasure and incidental profit, in much the same way Evelyn himself enjoyed coins. Casual as it is, the book does supply a vast quantity of numismatic facts. There are many lists: types of medals, forms of inscriptions, rare coins and those commonly available in England, counterfeits and suspicious marks to be noted, famous artists of coins and collections thereof, and outstanding Greek and Roman medals not cited by previous authorities. Evelyn describes methods of copying medals, arranging collections, mounting the coins for display, and caring for collections: employ a trained person, not the valet, is his advice. He

interprets inscriptions and abbreviations and explains the significance of dress, posture, gesture, and various symbols found on
medals. He discusses at length the English mints and the contemporaneous crisis caused by clipped coins. He details exhaustively the subjects found on the backs of coins and evaluates
many of these, sternly objecting to some medals as offensive in
their flattery and others as "*Sarcastical*" (99). He tells of the
use of "mock medals . . . so denominated from their help in sup-
putation" (41)—that is, counters with no currency value, used
for reckoning. And, among the unfamiliar materials for coins, he
notes, "We read, and have seen of *Paper Money* . . . Mention is
likewise made of *Shells* . . . *Pibbles* . . . nay Bones of human
Skuls . . . and other Bones are Traffick at this day among the
rude *Americans*" (11).

Probably the most curious and entertaining parts of the book
are digressions. One body of these is a list of nonexistent medals:
"What would one not give for the true Picture of the Hero's,
Heroines, and other illustrious Persons whom we have mention'd,
and that have made such a noise in the World?" (43). Not only
does he suggest people but also things and events—such items as
the column commemorating the Great Fire, the inventor of knit-
ting machines, the start of the penny post—scattered examples
that are only teasers. In Chapter 8, he settles down in earnest and
gives close to thirty pages of regrettably unminted subjects for
medals. Some pages have columns of lists naming individual law-
yers, judges, wits, musicians, travelers, and benefactors.

These listings are staggering because of the fertility of Evelyn's
mind and because of his seemingly inexhaustible *élan*. Plotters
and discoverers of plots, impostors, scholars, "celebrated Misses
and illustrious Strumpets," great eaters and great fasters, "the
Famous *Irish Gastrimuth* and *Ventriloquus Fanning*, our *Milo*,
(and other *Gastrimargi*)," great begetters and child bearers,
"*Babo* Earl of *Abensperg*, who being Father of Forty Children,
brought Two and Thirty of them, (all alive, and at once) to wait
upon the *German* Emperor . . . but above all, *Margarite* Countess
of *Honeberg*, who brought forth as many Children at one Birth,
as there are Days in the Year," and "any of the *Seven Sleepers*"
(266–67). Evelyn might well have applied here a phrase he uses
in a letter to Pepys, amid a disorderly list of prospects for a

painting collection: "I still recite them promiscuously & not like an Herauld" (Aug. 12, 1689).

There are two lists of poets, one English and later, when Evelyn gets a second wind, Continental celebrities. The English list, only half a page long, is impressively discriminating in its selection when one considers the judgment of posterity. A chronological analysis (the list is alphabetical) reveals a sharp leap from medieval to Elizabethan with a hiatus where such Tudor names as John Skelton, Thomas Wyatt, and the Earl of Surrey might be expected. Some minor Elizabethans are omitted—Thomas Campion, Joseph Hall, Walter Raleigh. And likewise some seventeenth-century figures, like John Marston, William Davenant, and Richard Lovelace.

Just how sensitive an ear and genuine appreciation Evelyn had for poetry is questionable. His remarks in the preface to his translation of Lucretius are shallow; his references in his diary are remarkably rare. The value of this list, therefore, is its evidence of his awareness not only of the importance of English poetry— he cites no other genre—but also of the best poets, whether the selection was his own or based on public consensus.

Toward the end of these prolific lists, Evelyn himself grows sufficiently self-conscious to say "And now I confess it may be wonder'd, why I should call over so extravagant a List of *Names*, and what my meaning is? since it were madness but to fancy that there should be found *Medals* of the hundredth part of all this *Bead-roll;* or that after all this, I would prostitute the Dignity of *Medal* (so much celebrated) with the *Effigies* of every rich Clown, or impertinent, who was able to be at the Charges of a *Stamp*" (288). Madness or no, the answer is simply the affirmation that medals may properly be made of anything, "some of all Capacities, signal for any Thing or Action extraordinary, and that possibly may enter into any part of History." It is not the medals but their subjects, or even more exactly their historical import, which is the true basis for Evelyn's interest.

The lengthy last chapter, "Digression concerning Physiognomy," is similarly justifiable by this view of medals as primarily a means to an end. In it, Evelyn sets forth his belief that "the Art of Divination from the Countenance, is a *Science*" (324), although he has earlier admitted "that the Countenance is not always an infallible Guide" (309). But with Bacon as his most immediate source, he outlines physiognomic study, interpreting the head feature by feature and then proceeding to the whole body. He entertains objections—considering, for example, "how it happens, that we often find so many of the fair, and beautiful Sinners of the Sex, in divers of whose Countenances there appears to dwell so much Innocency, Sincerity, Modesty and Goodness" (306)—and dismisses rather than answers them.

Evelyn often includes digressions within the digression. He relates anecdotes of curious behavior consequent upon extraordinary nursing in infancy; for instance, "*Scotus* tells of a Boy, nourished with the Milk of a *Sow*, that could never be reclaimed from running into Ditches and dirty Puddles" (312). He weighs the respective effects upon temperament of heredity and environment, particularly in terms of terrain and climate. He ends the chapter with a survey of celebrated men whose painted or medallic countenances accord with Evelyn's reading of their characters —Erasmus ("easy, pleasant facetiousness"), Thomas More ("great Probity . . . extraordinary Chearfulness"), Bacon ("a Soul in sublime Contemplation"), and Thomas Hobbes, in whose face Evelyn discovers "a supercilious, Saturnine *Opiniatrety*, pleased with himself" (341).

Numismata is a book that it is easy to scorn. Horace Walpole regretted the fact that Evelyn did not discuss the engravers and that he neglected the native artists. Walpole's tone is sharp, therefore, but his statement fairly perceptive when he says, "I should not have expected that a virtuoso so knowing would have contented himself with descriptions of the persons represented, he who had it in his inclination, and generally in his power, to inform posterity of almost every thing they would wish to know. . . . In short, Mr. Evelyn, who loved to know was too fond of telling the world all he knew." [8] Subsequent comments soften the asperity, for Walpole is just and sufficiently modest to recognize that some of his own work might, in fact, be "not much to the purpose."

Neither notably just nor modest but at least as amusing in his criticism of Evelyn was John Pinkerton who published an *Essay on Medals* in 1784. The preface surveys and cites the shortcomings of studies prior to his own. Of Evelyn's, Pinkerton wrote: "The size is folio, and the plan and writing are likewise in folio. None of his observations are new. . . . The plates of English medals are of little use. . . . Even they would have been better understood, had he not added explanations. There is, in the British Museum, a copy of this work, corrected by the author, with an original letter prefixed, complaining that the printer had utterly mangled and spoiled his work, so that it is necessary to give corrections. The corrections are for the worse." [9]

One may find fault with the errors, misprints, and irrelevance in which Evelyn indulges; or one may value the worth and minimize the defects. For the reader who presumes that coins and medals should be studied primarily as works of art, the focus of *Numismata* is disappointing. From first to last, Evelyn is quite consistent in his own thesis: the distinctive value of coins and medals is that they are the least perishable of historical records. He does not despise the artistry; but, as he says in a letter to Pepys, "all copies, if well dissembled, stamp'd, or cast, are not to be rejected" (Aug. 12, 1689).

Numismata was influential as an important forerunner and incentive for other histories of art. Evelyn's proposals for cataloguing medals were also a contribution. The value of the book today as a reference work is genuine but limited. It is useful, however, as a record of a vast quantity of seventeenth-century opinions, ideas, and taste. And it is amusing as an anthology of odd lore.

The older Evelyn grew, the more deeply he felt the mutability of things, most particularly the inroads time makes on man's better endeavors. This recognition prompted him to write an essay "Of Manuscripts," just as it had motivated those almost hysterical lists in *Numismata*. The date he composed "Of Manuscripts" is hard to determine, for the diary does not refer to it, and the internal evidence only indicates a date after 1685, as it speaks of "his late Mat^y K. Charles the 2^d." The essay remained in manuscript until William Bray included it in the first edition of the *Memoirs* in 1818. Evelyn states at the start that the essay is designed for those unfamiliar with manuscripts, "such as are lesse exercis'd and vers'd, but who are no lesse curious" (II, 335). How comprehensive a study he planned is not clear; he speaks of one or two chapters, but actually completed only one.

Of the approximately three thousand words which he did write, about a third are devoted to what he is not going to discuss: "Neither shall I charge this Chapter with so large a Recen-

sion of all those *Authors* whose Workes we have wholly lost, &
are perish'd, or of such whose Fragments onely remaine" (II,
336). He names some authors whose works are lost or fragmentary, and he describes subjects on which manuscripts are known
to have existed, interspersing his lists with exclamations of grief:
"so sad a Catalogue . . . inestimable losse . . . the publique losses.
. . . What shall we then say of Socrates, the wisest among them
all, as appears by those short & scanty extracts." And so he advises the collector that he treasure whatever he can acquire, even
if it be "onely fragments & single sheetes, on whatsoeuer subject" (II, 340).

The chapter then concentrates on the problem of reading manuscripts. Evelyn cites texts which help the beginner; and he speaks
briefly about alphabets, punctuation, ancient languages, the letters themselves, ancient shorthand systems, and the ornamentation of manuscripts. After a word about different kinds of ink and
paper, he ends with a recipe: "Take beaten Galls, and infuse
them in a glass of White Wine for a day"; then use the fermented
and distilled product to bring out "worne and dim'd" letters (II,
348).

It is a rare composition of Evelyn's that does not convey his
enthusiasm for his particular topic, although the feeling is often
not explicit. "Of Manuscripts" is distinguished by its sustained
earnestness. Too superficial to be very informative, the essay may
be read as something close to a rhapsody.

IV Acetaria

Forty years passed between Evelyn's first gardening book *The
French Gardiner* and his last, *Acetaria* (1699)—the first, a com-
petent but prosaic translation; the last, one of his most human,
curious, and amusing compositions. In *The French Gardiner* he
deliberately omitted Bonnefons' remarks on cookery, and he announced his own elaborate plan for a horticultural encyclopedia.
In *Acetaria*, his subject is entirely culinary; or to use the more
exact phraseology which he himself applies, the esculent uses and
qualities of various vegetables. And he announced the end of his
horticultural writing, acknowledging now that his "Plan of a
Royal Garden" would never be more than (1) the finished outline, which he includes here, and (2) this additional volume,
which is Chapter 20 in the "Plan." In a way, his grandiose scheme

had come to a paltry end. Yet, in terms of the interest and quality of *Acetaria,* it was a not unworthy epitome of a lifetime's learning—learning what is achievable and what purely visionary, what merit can be found in modest endeavors, and that a well-dressed salad is not to be despised in the scale of life's pleasures.

Evidently Robert Boyle had thought this way when he wrote the Royal Society in 1668 requesting information on herbs.[10] Boyle's salad days were well past by the time Evelyn compiled his answer, but the Royal Society was thriving; and Evelyn wrote a lengthy word of praise in the form of a dedication, providing a terse statement about the aims of the Royal Society. It sums up Evelyn's own belief: that "a shallow and superficial insight" has made many atheists, but "a profound and thorow penetration into her [nature's] recesses (which is the business of the Royal Society) would lead men to the knowledge and admiration of the glorious Author" (*Misc. Writ.,* 724–25).

Grasping this point of view is central to an understanding of Evelyn. The one synthesizing element in all his intellectual pursuits—more than any devotion to the king, to Royal Society, or to any plan to write a history of trades or *Elysium Britannicum*—is this divine final cause. Even the semijocular justification of his topic with which he ends the dedication is introduced with scriptural allusion: "I expect some will wonder what my meaning is, to usher in a trifle with so much magnificence, and end at last in a fine receipt for the dressing of a sallet with an handful of pot-herbs! But yet . . . he who wrote of the cedar of Libanus wrote also of the hysop which grows upon the wall" (725). He cites Pliny and Cicero as additional precedents and contrasts himself with Apicius, a notorious Roman epicure, claiming that his own interest is not "gratifying a Sensual Appetite with a Voluptuary *Apician* Art" (726). Indeed, he is a moderate eater and would not be misunderstood: "So as to this book-luxury, I can affirm, and that truly, what the Poet [Martial] says of himself (on a less innocent occasion), *Lasciva pagina, vita proba.* God forbid, that after all I have advanc'd in praise of sallets, I should be thought to plead for the vice I censure, and chuse that of Epicurus for my lemma" (727).

The preface is a brief but vehement attack on authors "who have arrogated, and given the glorious title of 'Compleat and

Accomplish'd Gardiners' to what they have publish'd, for Evelyn has not found "that ever any mortal man from Adam, Noah, Solomon, Aristotle . . . had ever arriv'd to the perfect knowledge of any one plant or vulgar weed whatsoever" (728). Since Evelyn had used, only six years before, such a title for his translation of de la Quintinye, his denunciation seems a bit strong; but this preface is really a prelude to "The Plan of a Royal Garden," the scope of which is so ambitious that no one man could in fact accomplish such a range. In a very few pages Evelyn lists the titles of the forty-two divisions, which he calls chapters but each of which could readily be a volume in itself.

The text opens with a discussion of cooked and raw vegetables, Evelyn's authority for using the term "Acetaria" for the raw, and the etymologies and definitions of each. Then comes an itemization of the "Furniture and Materials" of salads. Seventy-three kinds of plants are described in terms of what part of each is to be eaten, how it is to be prepared, and what nutritional values it has; and, after the list, there are general statements of the same nature. Finally satisfying Boyle's request, he gives a table of herbs, their ordering, culture, harvest, use, and seasonal features. The matter of salad dressing nominally occupies the final portion of the work, but Evelyn, evidently feeling no constraint, expatiates on such diverse topics as the temperamental differences of carnivores and vegetarians, the biblical prohibition against eating blood, the question of whether plant life has degenerated over the years, and the evils of undue fasting. An appendix gives a few recipes, including cowslip wine, which Evelyn recommends to accompany salads. The table of contents—an alphabetical index—consists largely of the names of vegetables, fruits, and spices; but there are glints of Evelyn's usual heterogeneity in such entries as

Abstemious Persons who eat no Flesh . . . nor were under Vows . . .
Alleluja . . .
Altar dedicated to Lettuce . . .
Children chuse to eat Fruit before other Meat . . .
Decay in Nature, none . . .
Man . . . not lapsed so soon as generally thought . . .
Monks and Friers perstring'd for their idle unprofitable life
Tulip eaten that cost 100£

What distinguishes *Acetaria* as one of the most pleasing of Evelyn's writings is the combination of unrestrained enthusiasm combined with great selection of material and economy of expression. It is a rare page which does not display the vitality and keen interest of the author as well as a succinct exposition of uncommon facts or folklore. The vocabulary is technically precise without losing its elegance. A frequent juxtaposing of homely details with Classical allusions provides a suitable dignity. Evelyn maintains his sense of humor and of values.

One can quote from almost anywhere to illustrate these points. He calls the artichoke "this noble Thistle" (736), and he reports that Carthage spent thirty thousand pounds annually on this vegetable. He informs us that "cresses, *nasturtium* . . . quicken the torpid spirits, and purge the brain . . . and the vulgar *Water-Cress* . . . best for raw and cold Stomachs, but nourish little" (739). Cucumber is "the most approved sallet alone" and is especially good if one does not make "the vulgar mistake of altogether extracting the juice, in which it should rather be soak'd" (739). He dwells at some length on the cucumber since it was not long since it was considered "little better than poyson" by the English —in contrast to "the Levant, [where] if a Child cry for something to eat, they give it a raw cucumber instead of bread" (740). Garlic is totally forbidden "by reason of its intolerable rankness" (741) owing to which, Evelyn has read, eating it was once a punishment "for such as had committed the horrid'st crimes" (742). Lettuce is incomparably beneficial, for it "bridles Choler, extinguishes thirst, excites appetite, kindly nourishes, and above all, represses vapours, conciliates sleep, mitigates pain; besides the effect it has upon the morals, temperance, and chastity" (743).

Evelyn is very dubious about mushrooms, for they seem to him at best "tolerable only (at least in this Climate)." Against him, however, is ancient opinion: "Exalted indeed they were to the second course of the Caesarian tables." On the other hand, their origins are suspect, "produc'd by the midwifry of autumnal storms," and their "funest" results have been immortalized by ancient poets: "He that eats Mushrooms many times *nil amplius edit*, eats no more perhaps all his life after" (746). In addition to the better-known plants, Evelyn cites such rarities and delicacies as alexanders, goats-beard, viper-grass, and turnip bread. He tells that he once experimentally concocted macaroons from sunflower seeds—not recommended, for "the turpentine did so domineer over all, that it did not answer expectation" (757).

As for the salads for which these acetaria are destined, the blending should be such that no one herb overpowers the others; for all should "fall into their places, like the notes in music, in which there should be nothing harsh or grating" (763). Then he gracefully acknowledges that the comparison is not original, and he balances the sublimity with humor by quoting Horace, Democritus, and others with their various comical and braggart cooks and then Milton with his punctiliously domestic Eve.

While Evelyn finds honorable precedent for his work, the topic was by no means a stale one at the time of his writing. The literary men to whom he refers introduced food only incidentally to other subjects. The only Classical work on cookery which has survived is that by Apicius; but, as has been noted, Evelyn scorned him as a "voluptuary." Probably he knew him only by reputation, for manuscripts of his book were rare and the first printings date from the eighteenth century. Moreover, the few salads described by him are rather different from Evelyn's. In the Middle Ages, references to salads are not entirely clear, for the term was used for many potpourris of minced meat, fish, or fruits. The etymologically minded draw inferences about medieval taste from the fact that the modern word "garbage" comes from "gerbe" meaning greens. Apparently, salads in Evelyn's sense pretty much date from the sixteenth or even the seventeenth century.

In Evelyn's own time, Bacon in *Sylva Sylvarum or a Naturall History* had something to say about vegetables which are best served raw and those to be otherwise prepared; Evelyn's friend Kenelm Digby was not above collecting recipes; and Bonnefons had a book on food, *Les Delices de la Compagne.* John Parkinson's *Paradise in Sole* (1629) treats the kitchen garden briefly; and Robert May, who wrote *The Accomplisht Cook* in 1660, includes grand salads in many of his bills of fare. Leonard Meager's *The English Gardiner* (1670) devotes a third of its pages to "Herbs for Salads," but mainly to their culture, with only two recipes. Closer to Evelyn in time and taste is Giles Rose, one of the master cooks in Charles II's kitchen and author of *A Perfect School of Instruction for the Officers of the Mouth,* 1682; but he gives only 15 pages to "Sallets for the four seasons of the year" out of 561 pages for the entire book.

[110]

Evelyn was, therefore, a pioneer in devoting an entire book to the subject. After him, books on food became fairly common; and some of them were so ridiculous that in 1708 there appeared an elaborate parody called *The Art of Cookery in Imitation of Horace's Art of Poetry* by William King, who laughed at the whole idea of such solemn concern over gastronomy. Evelyn's genial presentation and personal prestige may well have completed the entrenchment of the salad in English life and literature; at any rate, the book has continued to be esteemed.

V *Last Works*

While *Acetaria* was the last full book of Evelyn's to be published during his lifetime, and a worthy culmination it was, he published one more item after that, a brief affair with its origins far in his past. When Evelyn was in Padua in 1646, he attended the celebrated anatomy lectures there, observed surgical operations and dissections, "purchased those [two] rare Tables of *Veines* & *Nerves,* & causd him [a Dr. Leonius] to prepare a third of the *Lungs, liver,* & *Nervi sexti par:* with the *Gastric* vaines, which I transported into England, the first of that kind had ben ever seene in our Country, & for ought I know, in the World, though afterwards there were others" (Diary, Feb., 1646). In 1667, Evelyn presented these panels to the Royal Society. Thirty-five years later, when the Royal Society decided to make this material publicly available with engravings of the drawings, Evelyn wrote a letter telling how he bought the tables in Italy and gave them to the Royal Society. His letter appeared in the *Philosophical Transactions* of the Royal Society.[11] The only interest of the piece for students of Evelyn's work is its evidence of Evelyn's consistency: he had not tired at eighty-two of what had commanded his attention more than fifty years earlier.

Memoires for my Grand-son, Evelyn's last work, was not designed for publication and did not appear in print until the twentieth century. The dates of its composition are indicated within the text: it is headed 1704; near the end, Evelyn refers to his grandson's having taken a wife, an event which occurred in September, 1705, a very few months before Evelyn's death. The grandson addressed is John Evelyn III (eventually Sir John, the first baronet), a twenty-two-year-old at this time. Already as

Evelyn wrote, John III was the sole surviving male offspring bearing the family name, for he was the only living son of John Evelyn, Jr.; and John, Jr., the only one of John, Sr.'s sons to survive childhood, had himself died in 1699. In addition to the bond created by this heir apparency, John III's intimacy with his grandfather had been increased by his father's being in Ireland during part of the boy's school days and then by his father's illnesses; consequently, Evelyn had assumed a largely parental role with him. And a final endearment was the character of the boy himself, for he was steady, devout, able, and filial.

Although Evelyn refers to the book, near its close, as "undigested as for Method" (73), it is as orderly as anything he wrote, covering four topics at varying lengths. It opens with a description of Evelyn's will; it then briefly discusses devotion for the family and servants. The major portion is devoted to "Secular Concerns." At the end are fifteen pages of "Promiscuous Advices"—miscellaneous maxims, many of them copied from his own *Devotionarie Book.*

As has been noted before, Evelyn's minutely particularizing mind throve on details. When these are manifold or complex, his tendency to neglect generalizations and systematic ordering makes the minutiae tedious or even ridiculous. But, whenever he limited and selected the details, he produced a work of distinguished vividness. And when, as is usual, his own immense enthusiasm for these details shines through—what Geoffrey Keynes in his Preface to the *Memoires* calls "the admirable fussiness of the author" (xi)—the vitality becomes great. These merits characterize the *Memoires.*

For instance, when Evelyn proposes a budget for his grandson, one third of his income is to suffice for regular household expenses; one third, for savings and ultimately the education of the children; one third for extraordinary domestic demands (repairs, illness) and charity. One way to insure the working of this budget is the meticulous inventory and care of the tools, weapons, and other implements. Evelyn has little trust in unsupervised servants, for "they will squander things and sell them before your face, and pretend they are perquisits belong to their places, and imbezill goods before they are halfe worn out" (20).

Simply cataloguing the equipment seems to give Evelyn pleasure, for lists roll forth effortlessly and generously: "spade, Rake, sithe, water-potte, grassing Tooles, melon glasses, cases, Be-hives, Traps, Whet-stones, Reeles & lines, measures, forks, diblers, Trowelles, Brasses & things belonging to the fountains" (21). Every so often it occurs to Evelyn that the indispensability of an item or a practice may escape young John, and he then spells out the point: "A *Drum* is very necessary to give notice to your Neighbours upon any surprise by rogues, theives and fire, and [you] should therefore never beate it but on such occasions" (25–26). He is dogmatic on some practices and open-minded on others: there is no discussion but that the boat should "be lock'd and chain'd up, cauk'd and pitch'd before winter and the Aunings kepte cleane and dry," but whether there should be a door on the boathouse is debatable (26).

Evelyn, who feels the obligations of office strongly, impresses that view on his heir, urging him to seek and secure public positions and to fulfill them as well as he does his domestic duties. Evelyn's own annual entertainment of tenants is regularly noted in his diary, and he would not have less cordial treatment from young John: "To your *Tennants* be not strange or ridgid, difficult or exacting, & let none of them, if possible, go from you discontented" (35).

As for pastimes, Evelyn speaks briefly of recreations—he prefers chess and bowls to hunting—and devotes many pages to the studies which his grandson should pursue and in connection with which his library and museum will be of central importance. He assumes that his heir will read and collect books on such subjects as the sciences, law, history, geography, mathematics, arts, travels, and "all the Classics" (42). For languages, he finds it not too much to expect facility in Latin, Italian, French, Dutch, and Spanish. But chief among the studies is theology, including readings in church history, the early fathers, the reformers, sermon writers, and books of prayers.

While reading, the young man should keep a notebook, "A well digested *Adversaria* as to *common places* . . . in which to write down and note what you find most important & usefull in your Readings" (43). He will then refer to its contents when preparing speeches or other compositions, "no man being able to build any thing whatever without the help [of] others which may stand or last longer than the *Cobwebs* spun out of bowels of an Insect" (44). Yet twenty pages on he acknowledges that his own

Adversaria grew so "numerous and most of them superfluous, I left off" (63). In this connection, he spends several pages describing his own papers and advising how they are to be disposed of. The account is not exhaustive, but it contributes knowledge of his manuscripts and his methods.

When Evelyn advises that the museum attached to the library should be kept up, his detailed lists vividly illustrate again the wide reaches of Evelyn's taste and his indefatigability. He itemizes "Medalls, Intaglios, Coynes, Seales, modern Coines, &c. The Cabinet of natural Curiositys, that of the Drougs and Materia medica, Drawer of Seeds, Metalls, Minerals, Marcasite, Chonchs, shells, chrystals, stones, sparrs . . . small statues of plaster, wood, Glasses, Cups and other phantasticks, severall sorts of Lamps, Models, Moulds. Walking staves . . . All which should now and then be clensed from dust and other sullage" (54–55).

The *Memoires* is not the first document of this sort written by Evelyn. There are similarities with both *A Devotionarie Book* and the *Directions for the Gardiner,* but more relevant to the *Memoires* are the following pieces which still remain in manuscript. Shortly after marriage, he gave his wife "Instructions Œconomique," a survey of precepts and practices for a young married woman. For Margaret Godolphin, he wrote "Œconomics to a newly married friend." For his son, he prepared "an *Office,* with Instructions how to govern his Youth" (Diary, Dec. 23, 1677); and he wrote him, at the time of his marriage, lengthy letters that concentrate mostly on the hygienic and psychological reasons for some degree of sexual continence. He presented his daughter with "Directions for the employment of your time: for his daughter Mary." And, presumably under his tutelage, Mary wrote two memoranda of her own: "Rules for spending my pretious tyme well," and "Necessary additions to those Directions of my Father when I was at Sayes Court." [12]

One might say that Evelyn was almost habituated in writing advice and rules of life by the time he composed the *Memoires for my Grand-son.* It is the less surprising, therefore, that he makes no overt reference to precedent or authority, although he was undoubtedly thoroughly familiar with the many ancient and contemporary examples of the type. His work has enough in common with other seventeenth-century advices to warrant comparison; yet on almost every point it has individuality. It speaks across the gap of two generations rather than to a son. It covers moral, intellectual, and social matters, the usual range; but, unlike the other authors who tend to see their sons as morally shapeless, Evelyn assumes that young John has the appropriate virtues. And Evelyn does not preach and exhort, as is customary; he just suggests concrete applications. The typical seventeenth-century father who set pen to paper felt excessive study could be as destructive as insufficient; Evelyn expresses no fears that his grandson will either ruin his health or demean himself through pedantry. On the contrary, while he sees some need for recreation and exercise, here is where he urges moderation, preferring sedentary and intellectual pastimes.[13]

But even more than in these differences of emphasis or degree, *Memoires for my Grand-son* is essentially distinguished by its warmth, spontaneity, and particularity. Except in the collection of maxims at the end which are inevitably impersonal, Evelyn talks directly from experience, relates everything to life at Sayes Court and Wotton, expresses affection for his grandson, and indicates his great faith in him. He speaks everywhere with the voice of one well content with life, and what makes this last conviction so indisputably felt is the fact that it is never stated. For what protestations that life in general is worth the effort are needed from a man who, with his shaky and stiffened eighty-five-year-old hand, sets down the list of the gardener's tools—"Roller handles, Turn-cocks, Bird-netts, Matts, Baskets, Hamer, nailes, saw, hatchet, Bills, pruning knives, Water-levell"—exhorting his heir to enjoin the gardener never to "leave any of these moveable Tooles abroad in the night" (21). Whatever questions, if any, may have troubled Evelyn at earlier periods as to the value and future of his way of life, not a doubt dims the optimism of this document.

One might well corroborate Evelyn's own estimate of the work: "I conjure you therefore to Receive this . . . as one of the most valuable legacys I can leave you" (73). The phrase has a finality about it; Evelyn knew that this was the end of his literary career. In these last twenty years, he had appropriately maintained his role in respect to writing for the Royal Society; he had written three of his most attractive books, *Directions for the Gardiner*, *Acetaria*, and *Memoires for my Grand-son*; and he had completed or otherwise brought to conclusion all his major projects. He continued revising the *Silva-Terra-Acetaria* compendium, and the last edition of this work from his hand was published within months after his death. He made entries in his diary through February 3, 1706, and he died on February 27.

CHAPTER 5

The Correspondence and the Diary

IN the century following Evelyn's death, the notable biographical dictionaries and histories of the various arts perpetuated
his name by laudatory references and fancy epithets: "le petit
Milord Anglois," "The English Peiresc," "the philosopher of Wotton," and "Sylva Evelyn." His writings were his chief distinction,
and decorous critics applauded him as a polite author, learned,
able, and agreeable; and the most enthusiastic used such a phrase
as "another Virgil." *Silva* was reprinted several times from Evelyn's last edition (with *Terra, Pomona, Acetaria, Kalendarium
Hortense,* etc.) and then got a fresh lease on life from Alexander
Hunter's annotated reprint which somewhat altered and abridged
the text and added a life of Evelyn. Likewise reprinted—most of
them several times—were his *Sculptura* and *Fumifugium,* his
translation of Freart's *A Parallel* with his own *Account of Architects,* the London and Wise abridgment of the de la Quintinye,
and as parts of others' works his *Narrative of the Encounter, London Revived,* and *A Character of England.* Few years passed in
the eighteenth and early nineteenth centuries without his name
appearing in the lists of books just published and sometimes even
among the books reviewed.

Yet in a sense his literary identity, as one thinks of it today,
was still to come; for, except by a few members of the family and
even fewer friends, Evelyn's diary went unnoticed all this while.
An anecdote frequently reprinted is that of William Upcott's discovery that Evelyn's manuscripts at Wotton were being used by
Evelyn's great-great-grandson's family for kitchen wastepaper,
for patterns for dressmaking, and as general scrap paper. Through
Upcott's efforts and the work of William Bray, the first edition
was published in 1818: *Memoirs, Illustrative of the Life and
Writings of John Evelyn.* The contents are an incomplete version
of the diary, a selection from Evelyn's personal letters, a selection

from other correspondence which Evelyn owned, and a handful of other texts by Evelyn.

So successful was the diary that a standard set of Evelyn's works was issued by 1825: the two volumes of the *Memoirs* including the correspondence; *The Miscellaneous Writings,* the only collected edition that has been made of Evelyn's works; and a two-volume fifth edition of the entire *Silva.* Of all these materials, the *Silva* needs no comment here; the *Miscellaneous Writings* and the correspondence deserve some consideration; and the diary requires leisurely examination.

I The Miscellaneous Writings

William Upcott, who had worked on the diary, edited *The Miscellaneous Writings.* He chose the selections; provided a general introduction, brief prefaces to the individual works, and some notes; and supplied other texts, such as works which prompted or replied to Evelyn's. The contents are almost all of Evelyn's published books aside from the *Silva* volume; the only notable exception is the *Numismata.* Many of his essays are included, but Upcott omitted almost all the strictly occasional pieces (poems, prefaces, and some essays) and all the translations except the Chrysostom; however, he retained Evelyn's prefaces from almost all the translations. The volume is commendably selected and edited, although more explanatory material would be valuable for today's reader. This one collection of Evelyn's works was reprinted only once and then went out of print.

II *Correspondence*

Evelyn's correspondence was overshadowed by the bulk and interest of his diary; and his letters are still, today, the most neglected part of Evelyn's writings. There has never been a complete or indeed a separate edition, for the letters have been published only as a supplement to the diary or as part of other people's correspondence. No itemization of the epistolary manuscripts has been published or perhaps even completed. The actual number of letters by Evelyn, extant either as sent or as drafted in his letter book, has not been established. Judging by what has been published and by what authors with access to the manuscripts have cited, there seem to be around three hundred letters.[1]

By comparison with the eighteenth and subsequent centuries, the quantity is not vast; but it is ample to warrant attention.

The letters offer great variety in terms of the time period during which they were written, at least fifty years; the correspondents; the occasions for the letters; the subjects covered; and the lengths of the letters, from some of two hundred words to the six-thousand-word marathon sent to Pepys on August 12, 1689. The collection is sufficient to represent Evelyn both in opinion and style.

As one would expect, many of Evelyn's distinguished contemporaries are among his correspondents: the lord chancellor (Cornbury), the lord high treasurer (Clifford), Jeremy Taylor, Thomas Browne, Pepys, Thomas Sprat, Christopher Wren, Anthony à Wood, Richard Bentley, and William Wotton. Only slightly represented in the published correspondence are letters to his immediate family—his wife, brothers, children, and grandchildren—and intimate letters to such a close friend as Mrs. Godolphin. The occasion for his writing are the usual ones: condolence and congratulation, acknowledgments and thanks for honors and gifts, replies to requests for information in connection with books that others are writing, requests of his own for data for his books, reports on his fulfillment of obligations in his various offices, advice on travel and education and behavior, and simply exchange of news.

Several of the letters are genuinely essays in subject and form, the two most distinguished dealing with Evelyn's "proposal to Errect a (Philosophic) *Mathematical* College" (Diary, Sept. 1, 1659) and his plan for the improvement of the English tongue. These letters are typical of Evelyn at his most imaginatively prolific, highly particularized, and relatively practical; his tone is ebulliently optimistic that the plans will be implemented. The Philosophical College was to be a kind of Academy or Brook Farm, where scholars would live together under conditions austerely refining and presumably inspiring. The letter prescribes even such points as distribution of apartments; hours of rising (6:00 A.M.), prayer, and conversation; types of food, "plain and wholesome"; and recreation: "All play interdicted, *sans* bowls, chess, &c. Every one to cultivate his own garden" (to Robert Boyle, Sept. 3, 1659).

The letter planning the improvement of the language (to Peter

Wyche, June 20, 1665) discusses the sources of corruption of the language: "victories, plantations, frontieres, staples of com'erce, pedantry of schooles, affectation of travellers, translations, fancy and style of Court, vernility & mincing of citizens, pulpits, political remonstrances, theatres, shopps, &c." Evelyn suggests "a Gram'ar for the praecepts . . . a more certain Orthography . . . some new periods, and accents." He calls for many dictionaries, each for a different kind of word: pure, technical, exotic, dialectic, "ye most quaint and courtly," and archaic words. His last recommendation is that "there must be a stock of reputation gain'd by some public writings and compositions of ye Members of this Assembly, and so others may not thinke it dishonor to come under the test, or accept them for judges and approbators."

Obviously, some of Evelyn's letters are the product of carefully polished composition; but the more characteristic style is spontaneous. The sentences tend to be long and rambling, often to the point of disorderliness; but they are always lively and brisk in their effect. The tone is generally earnest with occasional passages of dry humor. The identity of the person addressed is so evidently before Evelyn, dictating the manner and treatment of the subject, that one obtains a clear sense of the relationship and of the personality of the recipient. The more informal letters are probably the nearest thing to be found that reflects Evelyn's way of thinking and perhaps even of talking.

Excerpting illustrations from the letters is not easy because Evelyn interweaves his ideas very closely, but some samples may be offered. For an example of his grandiloquent style, designed for a professor of rhetoric, a Mr. Croone, this passage suffices: "It has neither proceeded from the unmindfulnesse of y^r desires, or y^r deserts, that I had not long before this gratified y^r inclinations, in finding you out a condition, which it might become you to embrace, if you still continue y^r laudable curiosity, by wishing for some opportunity to travell, and see the World" (July 11, 1663). Earnestness and high style are combined in a letter of condolence to Jeremy Taylor: "If dividing and sharing greifes were like the cutting of rivers, I dare say to you, you would find your streame much abated; for I account my selfe to have a great cause of sorrow not onely in the diminution of the numbers of your joyes & hopes, but in the losse of that pretty person, your strangely hopeful Boy" (Feb. 17, 1658).

Speaking about his own writings in a letter to Richard Bentley, he displays openness of manner and grace of expression: "I confesse I am foolishly fond of these & other rustications, which had ben my swete diuersions during the dayes of destruction and devastation both of woods and buildings, whilst the rebellion lasted so long in this nation: and the kind receptions my bookes have found makes me the more willing to give them my last hand" (Jan. 20, 1697). And again to Bentley, Evelyn writes at Christmas time from Wotton about a design for a new library to be built in St. James's Park: "To send you notice of this, I thought might be much more acceptable to you than to acquaint you that we are full of company, & already enter'd into a most dissolute course of eating & indulging, according to the mode of ancient English hospitality . . . The D^r gave us a sermon this morning, in an elegant and trim discourse of the 39. Psalm, which I find had ben prepar'd for the court, & fitter for that audience than our poore country churches. After this you will not expect much intelligence from hence . . ." (Dec. 25, 1697). The few but well-chosen details convey the romantic scene. The wry ambiguity gives it realism with a flavor of humorous, slightly testy resignation to the holiday spirit. His diary reference to this same sermon is far more reserved, citing its "great learning and eloquence" (Dec. 26, 1697).

The letters to Pepys are especially distinguished by an easy familiarity. Mentioning the new lord treasurer, Evelyn writes, "Clifford (his predecessor) was, with all his other imperfections, a generous man, and, I very believe, of cleane hands; I am sure I was oblig'd to him. . . . Clifford had greate failings, but was gratefull and firme to his friend" (Dec. 5, 1681). In the same letter, he tells of a friend's having lost a manuscript that Evelyn once wrote on "how far a Gentleman might become learned by the onely assistance of the modern languages." The satire underlying such a proposal would have been appreciated by Pepys, even without Evelyn's elaboration of the point: "'t was written with a virtuous designe of provoking our Court fopps, and for encouragement of illustrious persons who have leasure & inclinations to cultivate their minds beyond a farce, a horse, a whore, and a dog, which, with very little more, are the confines of the knowledge and discourse of most of our fine gentlemen and beaus."

Evelyn's humor, especially when directed to Pepys, is generally mildly self-deprecating. Answering some questions on music posed by Pepys, Evelyn writes, "you'l not be displeas'd at what he [Vossius, a member of the Royal Society] tells us of a certaine harmonie produc'd by the snapping of carters' whips, us'd of old at the feasts of Bacchus & Cybele; . . . and then speakes of a Coachman at Maestricht who plays severall tunes with his lash. To a lover of music and harmonie I could not omit this scrap, tho I know you'l laugh at me for it, & pay me with the tongues and gridiron" (Sept. 23, 1685).

Evelyn's correspondence ranks among the more important seventeenth-century collections, and contains information, ideas, lively descriptions of contemporary scenes, many amusing passages, and interesting variations in style. Hopefully, it some day will be available in a proper edition.

III   The Diary

Overshadowing all Evelyn's other literary endeavors and rightly so, in terms of its interest, length, range, uniqueness, is his diary. The monumental publishing success which it achieved is a matter of record, with edition following edition, each vastly enlarged over its predecessors, many augmented with annotations and introductions, and each edition running to many printings in America as well as in England. Magazines (English, French, Italian) included and even serialized parts. The Bohn Library, Universal Chandos Classics, and Everyman included the diary in its sets of reprints. A reaction against the many-volumed texts took the form of cheap editions and new selected editions. Certain sections were reprinted as separate books with titles of their own. An 1896 review, in discussing both Evelyn and Pepys, reports that "Half-a-crown or less spent at a railway bookstall or stationer's shop will now procure the Memoirs of either exhaustively indexed." [2]

The culmination of all this interest and of thirty years of research and editing by Esmond de Beer was the appearance in 1955 of *The Diary of John Evelyn, now first printed in full from the manuscripts;* the entire text is six volumes, with a comprehensive introduction, annotation, and index; and it is one of the outstanding pieces of editorial work of the twentieth century. Errors of previous texts are corrected, puzzling abbreviations and the like are explained, alterations and additions are set right, and everything that was omitted now appears. These previous omissions were prompted, Mr. de Beer tells us, by such varied considerations as "lack of interest, privacy, indelicacy, unintelligibility" or by the desire "to shorten [passages] or to improve their style,"—mainly notes of sermons, meetings of the Royal Society, family affairs, and some rather explicit medical details.[3]

The title "Diary" which the work now bears is not a precise designation, but no more is "memoirs" or Evelyn's own terms "vita" and "kalendarium"; for the final product is a combination of all of these. Evelyn, following the custom of his father, began making entries in an almanac when he was about ten years old. During his Grand Tour, he kept a fairly elaborate journal; and, when he returned to England, he resumed his brief notes, recording his engagements and other items of interest. Just when he wrote and expanded these original versions is unknown, but at intervals, from the late 1640's through the early 1680's, the two techniques were his practice: that is, jotting fairly rough, brief, abbreviated notes every few days and then retrospectively revising these, adding new details not known earlier and occasional generalizations and hindsights. From the mid-1680's onward, he kept a fairly full journal which stands pretty much in its original form. The work therefore comes to us partly as autobiography or memoirs and partly as a true diary or journal.

In yet another sense, all of these terms are misleading. For the work is not primarily personal, either in events or in response. Such personal details as Evelyn gives form a fractional part of the whole, and the major substance of the diary is almost a chronicle, giving accounts of public events, mention of famous people, descriptions of distinctive customs of the day, and records of singular occurrences and curiosities. Evelyn was in a favored position to witness many public events, to take his part in them, to observe and meet the celebrities of the day, and to report diligently on all of them. From the days of Charles I through the enthronement of Anne, it is a rare public occasion that is not at least acknowledged by Evelyn; and some he presents at length: the execution of Charles I, the funeral of Oliver Cromwell, the arrival of Charles II, the king's taking a wife and many a mistress, antipopery riots, fireworks for royal births and birthdays, the pillorying and whipping of Titus Oates, the great tax robbery of

1692, and battles with the Dutch which occurred just off the English coast. Many of these entries re-create the event impersonally, but they haphazardly evoke the tumult of the scene and give an immediate, spontaneous view.

Best known among the historical scenes are Evelyn's firsthand, detailed accounts of the Plague of 1665 and of the Great Fire of 1666. In the thick of both of these, he kept informed about developments, served where he could, and experienced anguish for the suffering and loss involved. Evelyn's details are not always reliable, as de Beer's annotation shows; but the discrepancies are not substantial. The following sequence of diary entries is typical, starting with August 28, 1665:

The Contagion growing now all about us, I sent my *Wife* & whole family (two or three of my necessary Servants excepted) to *Wotton* to my Brothers, being resolved to stay at my house my self, & to looke after my Charge, trusting in the providence & goodnesse of God. *September* 5 I went to (*Chattam*) to inspect my Province, carrying in my Coach 900 pounds [as Commissioner for Sick and Wounded Seamen, Evelyn had to see to the plague-stricken men in the Navy] . . . 7 Came home, there perishing now neere ten-thousand poore Creatures weekely: however I went along the Citty & suburbs from *Kent streete* to St. *James's*, a dismal passage and dangerous, to see so many Cofines exposd in the streetes & the streete thin of people, the shops shut up, & all in mournefull silence, as not knowing whose turne might be next: I went to the D: of *Albemarle* for a Pestship, to waite on our infected men, who were not a few: 10: Dr. *Plume* at Greenwich, on 3. Coloss: 5. 6. shewing how our sinns had drawne downe Gods Judgements: I dined with the Commissioners of the Navy, retreated hither, & with whom I had buisinesse.

The de Beer notes state that the London Bill of Mortality lists 8,252 deaths in the week ending September 5, only 6,988 of which are from plague: Evelyn's statement is an exaggeration and might easily be read to mean that the death figures refer only to plague victims. Yet this kind of inaccuracy is so normal a manifestation of excitement or involvement or haste, especially in combination with Evelyn's simplicity and random order of presentation, that the effect is a stark exposition of what living through these cataclysms was like.

Besides the singular public events, Evelyn also noticed more ordinary manners and pastimes. He tells of such entertainments as orations by the boys at Westminster School in Latin, Greek, Hebrew, Arabic; the pleasures of Mulberry Garden and of Spring Garden; displays of horsemanship and mock sieges, performed by the princes; the lord mayor's show; Christmas revels; tiger-, horse-, bull-, and bear-baiting; gambling; and royal "luxurious dallying." He describes the fashions in clothes; the hours, kinds, and quantities of food and drink served on various occasions; and also the declarations of public fasts.

A range of public attitudes and behavior appears in the references to public executions; the new custom of ministers' reading (rather than reciting or freely preaching) their sermons; the growing distaste for religious services, even to people's taking "Physick on the Lords day" to avoid churchgoing; a book-burning; "many bloody & notorious duels"; child-marriages in aristocratic families and an occasional lower-class wedding (so gracious were the Evelyns and so mobile was society becoming); a new tax on bachelors; and the paving of the Haymarket "which was a quagmire."

At times, he gives specific figures—the price of corn in many years, a royal loss of one hundred pounds at dice, and two thousand pounds paid for an election banquet by George Evelyn. And there are revealing vignettes of the interruption of a service by a debtor fleeing into church for sanctuary, levees and other informal visits to the apartments of royalty and the royal mistresses, and the "barbarous Costome" in country households whereby the resident staff entertained visitors' servants with so much refreshment that the coachman would become too drunk to drive his master and family home.

Evelyn had an acute sense of what was remarkable in an event or scene, and many of his notations are of innovations. He records the advent of sedan chairs; coffee, tea, and jacolatte (chocolate); the King-pine (pineapple); tobacco; public libraries; new branches of the service (grenadiers and dragoons); aristocratic ladies' painting their faces; stories of witchcraft from New England. He mentions the first divorce case at Westminster since Henry VIII; an experiment of printing a profile by means of "a dark large box," an early form of the camera; the introduction of such frivolities as ice skates and of violin accomplishment at church services; and the restoration of the communion table and rail.

He notices an extraordinary increase in robberies, highwaymen, and murders. He describes the custom of river bathing with tents "spread on the Water" for the ladies' privacy. Over the years, he reports on various surgical operations and new treatments for diseases and when "His *Majestie* began first to Touch for the Evil" (July 6, 1660). And he records notable eccentricities of the weather—droughts, severe cold, prolonged frost, storms—and he also suitably aligned these with divine providence and public depravity.

Next to significant political and social history, the most fascinating recurrent material in the diary is the product of Evelyn's inexhaustible curiosity—his record of seemingly every oddity, strange phenomenon, and freak that he saw or heard about. His personal motto was "Omnia explorate, meliora retinete"—explore all things, retain the better. Characteristically, Evelyn started from Scripture when he devised the motto; then he made a substitution—Paul had "prove all things" (I Thess. 5:21) rather than "explore"; and then he applied his explorations and retention to the whole range of human experience rather than limiting it to the moral.

This almost indiscriminate curiosity appears in the diary as soon as Evelyn's travels began: he reports a woman twenty-five times married, "yet it could not be proved, that she had ever made any of her husbands away" (Aug. 24, 1641); a monstrous fish caught in a well; a celestial phenomenon, which he calls a "shining clowd" in his diary (March 10, 1643) but describes thus in his *Vita*, "The Garden and Vineyard [of Lord Salisbury's House] very finely Watered, was worth seeing: But what was a more Extraordinary Sight, was a shining Meteor that Evening & night, resembling a naked Sword, bright like the Moone, pointing to the North, very dreadfully"; [4] a kitten (born on Evelyn's own bed in an inn, as he slept) with six ears, eight legs, and two bodies from the navel downward; a dromedary; a rope-dancer; a "Water Spouter," whose secret Evelyn bought; and a fraudulent alchemist.

His wonder at these spectacles is expressed in the same tone as his response to memorable persons, architectural glories, or scientific facts. The following excerpts from a day in Leyden are typical:

The Churches are many, and very faire. In one of them lyes interr'd that Prodigy of Learning, the noble & illustrious Joseph Scaliger, without any extraordinary inscription. . . . But amongst all the rarities of this place I was much pleasd with a sight of their Anatomy Schole, Theater & Repository adjoyning, which is very well furnish'd with Naturall curiosities; especially with all sorts of Skeletons. . . . The Skinns of Men & Women tentur'd on frames & tann'd: Two faire and entire Mummies . . . [and] I could not forget that knife which they here shew'd us, newly taken out of a Drunken Dutchmans gutts, by an incision in his side, after the sottish fellow had swallow'd it, when tempting to make himselfe vomit, by tickling his throat with the handle of it, he let it slip out of his fingers into his stomac, and had it taken out againe by the operation of that dextrous Chyrurgeon, whose Picture is together with his Patients preserv'd in this excellent Collection. (Aug. 27-28, 1641)

Lest one think that this record was just the product of the tourist's preoccupation with the outlandish, one may read on in the diary and find a white raven and a porcupine worthy of record in England; Siamese twins at a Southwark fair; the thigh bone of an "Ostridge" which "I much admired"; a ring-tailed lemur, discussed at greater length than the birth of his fourth son, which precedes it; a hairy maid, with "a most prolix beard, & *mustachios* . . . exceeding long" and hair on arms, neck, breast, and back; an exotic costume made of phoenix wings, seen in a London musem; live Virginia rattlesnakes; a woman "6 foote 10 Inches" tall whom Pepys records as being only six feet five; a fire-eater; a Garden of Paradise, animated with painted cutouts which moved, flew, crawled, and roared; a pious shipwright neighbor who prayed nightly in his own coffin; Quakers, "a new phanatic sect" whom Evelyn visited a prison to see; Italian eunuchs and the concerts they gave; the first unicorn brought to England (a rhinoceros).

Evelyn encouraged conversations about marvels; and friends, neighbors, and some of the periodicals to which he subscribed shared his attitude or at least gratified it. The queen mother, Henrietta Maria, gave examples of the sagacity of dogs; ladies-in-waiting told of a ghost that appeared in the palace; and others brought to his attention a quiet, seemingly unfanatical servant maid who broke out in red cross-shaped rashes on her arms (recalling to Evelyn the nuns of Loudun). With friends, he went to visit "a gallant Widow a Farmoresse, & I think of *Gygantic* race." But he could report only secondhand on a little Dutch boy with the letters "Deus meus" imprinted around the iris of one eye and "Elohim" around the other.

Returned travelers told him of biblical ruins near Nineveh and of an "attempt of the Nor-west passage" which was blocked by ice "blew as a Saphire & as transparant." The Royal Society satisfied and encouraged Evelyn's taste for the exceptional with its experiments with animals, plants, and mechanical inventions; and the diary often describes these meetings. In his later years, Evelyn was less likely to go out of his way to see rarities; but, at fifty-eight, when viewing Elias Ashmole's library, he was as taken by a toad embedded in amber as by the manuscript collection; at seventy-eight, he enjoyed examining a Chinese barber's portable shop at Gresham College.

It is easy to infer that the intellectual life of a man so easily diverted has probably no more than the appearance of profundity at best. But this opinion is precisely to ignore the milieu which is the background for his many diary entries. The first feature of this environment is the deliberately encyclopedic scope of interests pursued by almost every learned man; Evelyn was no exception. Coming as he did at the very beginnings of specialization and of the sudden proliferation of experimentation, he was enough part of the emerging world to treasure facts but not enough to see that it would no longer be appropriate for any man to take, like Bacon, all knowledge as his province. The number and variety of subjects of his formal writings are only another manifestation of this attitude which the modern mind may label promiscuous but the ancient, medieval, and Renaissance mind called universal.

Another point about Evelyn's curiosity is that, so relatively limited was the body of scientific data and so suddenly in the immediately preceding century and a half had many unimaginable facts been established (global world, heliocentric universe, microscopically viewed life, exotic lands and civilizations), that not only the distinction between fact and fancy but the whole question of what was ordinary and what extraordinary had to be completely re-examined. Surveying seventeenth-century scientific writing, one gets the impression that the abnormal was often considered more significant than the normal: so much the more reason for collecting every oddity, no matter how apparently trivial, for only thus could the genuinely unique be discriminated. The genius—Francis Bacon, Isaac Newton, John Locke, possibly Thomas Hobbes—had an intuition about these things and gave firm direction to the new investigations. Evelyn was not a genius, but he was an intelligent man; and he accepted the new view that the intelligent man's function was precisely that of rejecting the categorical attitudes of the past and of suspending generalization and judgment while collecting all the data possible.

And one final point perhaps deserves at least a glance. A modern psychologist might emphasize some more devious drive behind the pursuit of certain of these abnormal instances, associating the interest in monstrous births and farfetched bodily contortions and feats with Evelyn's ability to watch, more-or-less equitably, anatomy sessions, unanesthetized patients undergoing surgery, galley slaves working and being auctioned, and a prisoner being tortured. But, even were there a degree of morbidity involved—whether masochistically proving his own manliness or satisfying a streak of sadism, both very possible impulses in such a disciplined and sober citizen as Evelyn—the larger motivation and surely the more abiding one, accounting for the interest in both sideshow freaks and Royal Society experiments with vacuum tubes, is Evelyn's universal curiosity, simultaneously encyclopedic and experimental.

The final substantial element of the diary to be considered is Evelyn's treatment of personal material. There are quantities of facts and events: marriages, births, deaths, excursions, religious activities of the family, honors from royalty and other aristocracy, Evelyn's appointments to public offices, guests entertained and visits paid, hunting and hawking parties, legal involvements and parochial charities, conversations with the king and convivial gatherings with friends like Pepys or Wren or Margaret Godolphin.

Lengthier anecdotes appear from time to time, and these profit from Evelyn's gift for suspense and pertinent detail. He describes in leisurely fashion his brief military career (*Vita,* I, 27–28), an "Adventure en Cavaliere" among bellicose French peasants (May 7–12, 1650), a seven-day wait at the seaside for his wife to arrive from France (June 4–11, 1652), robbery by cutthroats near Tunbridge (June 23–July 15, 1652), the near-strangulation of his son Richard on a mutton bone (Dec. 31, 1654), yachting with

the King (Oct. 1–5, 1661), and the Four Days' Battle of June 1666
—"Being in my Garden I hearing the Greate gunns go thick off:
I immediately tooke horse, & rod that night to *Rochester*" (June
1–17, 1666). He tells of discovering Grinling Gibbons, the wood
carver (Jan. 18–Mar. 1, 1671) and of going on an autumnal
sporting party (Oct. 9–20, 1671) and a journey to the Northampton Assises improbably complicated by clandestine love affairs
(July 8–16, 1675). Among the tragic events are the death and
burial of his son Richard (Jan. 27–Feb. 17, 1658), of Mrs. Godolphin (Sept. 3–18, 1678), and of Mary Evelyn (Mar. 7–16, 1685);
the trial of Lord Stafford (Dec. 2–12, 1680); and the elopement
and death of his daughter Elizabeth (July 27–Sept. 2, 1685). Less
solemn but similarly detailed are an account of an unwelcome
assignment as matchmaker (May 16, 1681), the tale of a mys-
teriously affluent young man (Apr. 22, 1694), and a quarrel with
the rector of Wotton—Evelyn's own appointee—about his sermon
on "pride & Luxurie of Apparell, which could be applyed to none
save my Wife & Daughter," as they were the only gentry present
(July 18, 1703).

Occasionally Evelyn supplies intimate details. He mentions
when Mary Evelyn first felt life in her womb with the second
child. He frequently refers to the sufferings and treatments he
underwent with hemorrhoids and constipation. He is unusually
frank in giving his own unvarnished estimate of his nephew John
and of his marriage (which Evelyn had himself arranged).

But many facts are not supplied. Several of the books he wrote
are never mentioned at all in the diary, and for very few of them
does he give any information about the process of composition.
Notes on what books he read and his judgments on them went
into his commonplace books and are not mentioned in the diary.
The precise dates and titles of his offices are not all given. Specific financial information is almost totally lacking. He tells when
he ordered and received his first coach, but most of his household
possessions and art collection get no mention.

Many such details would be valuable primarily as facts of social history, but some would in themselves be amusing. But even
so interesting and provoking an experience as the renting of
Sayes Court to Tsar Peter the Great of Russia receives a discreet
treatment. At the time, Admiral John Benbow was tenant at
Sayes Court, and the negotiations were made between him and

the English king, William. Evelyn, living in Wotton, was not involved in the arrangements. He wrote in the Diary for February 6, 1698: "The Czar Emp: of *Moscovy,* having a mind to see the Building of Ships, hired my House at Says Court, & made it his Court & palace, lying & remaining in it, new furnish'd for him by the King." Noting the tsar's departure on April 21, Evelyn does not mention what he had already heard of the uncouth conduct of his royal guest.

So destructive was the tsar's way of life that Benbow petitioned the king, who ordered reports to be made on the garden, the house, and the furnishings. Benbow received damages for his furniture; Evelyn, for the property. The note to the diary, supplied by Mr. de Beer, tells us: "The traditional account is that Peter amused himself by riding in a wheelbarrow through the holly hedges" (Diary, V, 290, n. 6). But no details and little emotion are expressed in Evelyn's diary account: "[June] 9 [1698] I went to Deptford to view how miserably the Tzar of Moscovy had left my house after 3 moneths making it his Court, having gotten Sir Cr: Wren his Majesties Surveyor & Mr. London his Gardener to go down & make an estimat of the repairs, for which they allowed 150 pounds in their Report to the L: of the Treasury."

And, generally, the glimpses are few and dim when it comes to self-revelation, the acknowledgment of foibles and vanities, and the clarification of inner sentiments and judgments, hopes and fears. His grief at his infant sons' deaths is stated with a convincing gruffness but no expatiation, and this passage contrasts with the moving eulogy prefixed to his translation of Chrysostom. The agonized accounts of the deaths of Margaret Godolphin and of his daughter Mary are the exception. Months pass without any mention of his wife, much less of his feelings toward her. His annual self-evaluations on his birthday are expressed in language which is totally conventional and hence impersonal.

If one were to judge by the diary, Evelyn's one sin of sufficient consequence to be remembered is being surprised by sleep at Sunday afternoon services. His anxieties are always in terms of the general public welfare or general family affliction, never individual. His rare expressions of pleasure or satisfaction are most often prompted by superficial, conventional, or impersonal circumstances—a favor from great persons, a spell of agreeable

weather, reception of the sacrament, a fine sermon, or a successfully completed demonstration at a Royal Society meeting.

The initially wholehearted approval given the diary has not
continued to be the universal estimate.[5] Some readers have
doubted Evelyn's sincerity; others, his capacity for any great
feeling. And some have little to say for what the book does provide, so busy are they lamenting what it lacks: the kind of material which gives them hearty enjoyment in reading Pepys or Bos-
well. All of this commentary brings to the fore the question of
what criteria—literary and otherwise—apply to the genre of diary
or autobiography: what relevance has factual content to literary
effect? What part is played by the diarist's handling of it? Is passing judgment on the man permissible, and is this separable from
evaluating the diary? If it is, then what evaluative criteria are
to be used? These questions are basic yet easy to ignore in the
presence of the vividly phenomenological details of human activity.

For the first seventy-five years after its publication, commentators on Evelyn's *Memoirs* reviewed only the man, not the book.
Each considered different qualities—his intelligence, urbanity,
ideas, virtue, learning, contribution to the arts, amiability—but
all who praised the book did so because they found Evelyn exemplary in one or more of these respects. The exceedingly minor
voices of dissent made the same approach, for these critics were
preoccupied with Evelyn's regrettable taste for formal gardens or,
as heterodoxy became more vocal, with his solemnity, his complacency, his loftiness. When Pepys's *Diary* was published and
overtook Evelyn's in popularity, comparisons ensued; but it was
still the men, not their works, that were evaluated: Evelyn was
judged the more admirable; Pepys, the more likable.

Some critics, besides appreciating Evelyn as a person, praised
him as chronicler and social historian. Robert Southey analyzed
this element thus: "Journals and books of travels are among those
works which acquire by time more value than they lose: they are
the subsidiaries of history, and preserve the memory of many
things which history disdains to notice, as trifling while they are
trivial, but which become objects of curiosity when they are ob-
solete and ancient." [6] This criticism is a far less personal type,
but it still does not utilize literary criteria.

At the turn of the century, the emphasis shifted. Complaints were formulated about Evelyn's lack of humor, his lack of frankness. The consciousness grew that, while diarists are perhaps not free in the same sense as authors of fiction, they are deliberately selective; in fact, they have a certain creative potential in respect to their material. Seeing the implications of this view with unprecedented acuteness, one critic wrote that "Evelyn's own diary . . . is a most valuable repository of sights and things at home and abroad; but it is photographic, it lacks distinction and temperament. . . . He maps out rather than paints his stormy, stirring periods. His own individuality does not modify or tinge his theme." [7] The judgment is wrong—Evelyn's individuality marks everything he writes—but the right demand was being made.

From such a critical comment it was only a step to see the essential nature of the diary and, for the gifted critic, to set straight, graciously and definitively, why one likes what one likes and why one is not without reservations about the work. Austin Dobson made clear that the selection Evelyn exercises is intrinsic to his character and is directly accountable for both the good and ill effects in his work.[8] Richard Garnett focused his judgment very exactly thus: "But for Pepys's amazing indiscretion and garrulity, qualities of which one cannot have too little in life, or too much in the record of it, Evelyn would have been esteemed the first diarist of his age. Unable for want of these qualifications to draw any adequate picture of the stirring life around him, he has executed at least one portrait admirably, his own." [9] Whatever else may be said, the John Evelyn of the diary is an unmistakable personality.

Some critics have denied Evelyn's impact or failed to see it because they equate diary writing with introspection and soul baring. Such exercises were not for Evelyn. He not only saw no occasion for pouring forth his inner self but also, one infers, felt no call to explore it privately in any but the most routinely religious fashion. And there is nothing extraordinary in his attitude, considering his milieu. Pepys was the odd one in finding his personal vagaries so interesting as to warrant elaborate recording. Only in the faintest way had the trend begun of presuming that a man's inmost heart is his most identifying and fascinating feature, that introspection is a valuable exercise, and that idiosyncrasies and specific personal failings must be part of the portrait, whether the painting is to hang in one's closet or in the public gallery. This presumption produces its own sort of good works, but it is not the indispensable element of a diary.

The creation of the narrator and the delineation of his world form the essence of diary writing. With what degree of intimacy that narrator is revealed, whether or not one approves of him or of the values with which he informs his world, how exactly his descriptions correspond with contemporary events, and similarly how closely the narrator's persona and the diarist's personality seem to coincide—all these, valuable questions though they may be, are extrinsic to the artistry of the diary—as they are with any other literary genre. What is central is not that the narrator is real but that he is sufficiently realistic to evoke a response from the reader; that this narrator by his selection and arrangement creates an environment of his own and interprets it; and hence that the whole complex has verisimilitude, unity, power, and significance—like any other piece of literature. To the degree that these qualities are achieved, the diary is successfully and genuinely literary.

In large measure, Evelyn does achieve such characteristics. The narrator is a strong personality, clearly discernible. The confusion of criteria applied to the work and the critics' gusto, whether in praise or dissatisfaction, show this. However, the portrait of his age is not so successful as that of himself. One need read very few pages to see the striking differences between Evelyn's world and that depicted by any of his contemporaries who wrote autobiographically (Pepys, Anthony à Wood, Dorothy Osborne Temple, John Bunyan), even though they describe many of the same people, times, and places. But Evelyn often lacks the concentration and economy which give focus and power; and he supplies too many facts without comment: at times, the reader not deeply versed in seventeenth-century society and history must rely very heavily on footnotes to perceive anything beyond names and titles; even then, he may get no special sense or flavor from a scene. Almost any page taken at random illustrates this weakness and also provides a compensatory passage in which the scene vibrates with feeling and meaning. For example, here are portions of Evelyn's entries about a week-long excursion escorting the English ambassador and his entourage to

Dover for departure to France. The month and year are November, 1675:

9 I din'd at *B[erkeley] house,* & went late home: the next day being the time appointed for my L: Ambassador to set forth, (10) I met them with my *Coach* at *New-Crosse*: There was with him my Lady his Wife, & my deare friend *Mrs. Godolphin* who, out of an extraordinary friendship, would needes accompany my Lady to *Paris* & stay with her some time, which was the chiefe inducement of my permitting my *Sonn* to Travell . . . Thus we set out 3 *Coaches,* 3 Wagons, and about 40 horse besides my *Coach;* It being late and my Lord but *valetudinarie* yet, we got but to *Dartford* the first day . . . 13 at *Dover* Mrs. *Godolphin* delivered me her Will, which her *Husband* had given her leave to make . . . then after prayers, (14) the next morning . . . (it being *Sonday*-morning and a glorious day) We tooke solemn leave of one another upon the *Beach,* the Coaches carrying them into the sea to the *Boats,* which delivered them to Cap: *Gunmans Yacht* the *Mary;* & so I parted with my Lord, my sonn, & the person in the world whom I esteemed as my owne life Mrs. *Godolphin;* being under saile, the Castle gave them 17 Gunns, & Cap. *Gunman* answered with 11.¹⁰

No word is wasted in the account of the aristocratic progress across Kent and the details of the embarkation; therefore, the scene is easily visualized. Evelyn's deep feelings about the occasion are equally evident, even without the realization which comes ten pages later that Evelyn at that time did not know that Margaret Godolphin was secretly married (the reference to her husband shows that Evelyn wrote or revised the passage some time after March, 1676). The whole sequence is affective.

Then come these entries: "16 To Rochester, lay at the *Majors.* 17 returned home Blessed be God: 19 *Lond:* return'd: 21 our *Viccar* 7 *Matt.* 21. *Curate* I. *Gen:* I. the power of God in Creating & consequently preverving: 22 Lond: buisinesse at the Doctor Commons for my *Lady Tuke.* 28: *Coram Rege* Dr. *LLoyd* on 53 *Psal:* 11 on the final Judgement &c: 28 Communion at St. Jame's Advent Sonday: 30 Royal Society *Anniversary* Ellection, the fellows all dining together *more solito.*" The altered pace is indicative of Evelyn's frame of mind, that is true; but now the names and precision about facts hold little interest. The voice of Evelyn does not always infuse the picture with the wanted forcefulness.

Granting then that the very positive personality of John Evelyn

emerges in his diary and that the portrait of his times, while sometimes mechanical and colorless, is often alive and sometimes
really brilliant, the individual reader is still entitled to say
whether or not he likes all this. This is a judgment based on taste,
but it is nonetheless a valid judgment. Today, the accuracy and
inaccuracies of Evelyn's record have been almost completely established. The value of his diary as a reference work has been
agreed upon. The main points of its artistic strengths and weak-
nesses have been set forth. So the final judgment becomes, as with
every piece of art, a matter of taste.

Some critics already quoted responded negatively. Probably
the most discerning and winning phrasing of a favorable reaction
is that by Virginia Woolf in an essay written for the tercentenary
of Evelyn's birth. Listing, first of all, what can be held against
him—"he was not an artist; no phrases linger in the mind; no
paragraphs build themselves up in memory"—she is the more
convincing for the almost grudging way that she grants that his
nonartistry is, in its own peculiar way, "an artistic method this of
going on with the day's story circumstantially. . . . All through
his pages good men, bad men, celebrities, nonentities are coming
into the room and going out again. The greater number we
scarcely notice; the door shuts upon them and they disappear.
But now and again the sight of a vanishing coattail suggests more
than a whole figure sitting still in a full light." More than that,
states Miss Woolf, "our affections settle here or there"; and she
briefly lingers over this character and that vignette until she is
ready to sum up the performance—hers, and Evelyn's—by glimps-
ing, "Evelyn himself most of all, grown old, walking in his garden
at Wotton, his sorrows smoothed out, his grandson doing him
credit, the Latin quotations falling pat from his lips, his trees
flourishing and the butterflies flying and flaunting on his dahlias
too." [11]

But, coming full circle in this evaluation, one may now recon-
sider the importance in this work of the factual content. Acknowledging that the diary is more intelligible and unified than are the
events recorded and that it has a significance beyond that of the
events, one must also acknowledge that its appeal is inseparable
from its basis in reality. Were one to learn tomorrow that there
never was any Samuel Pepys and the shorthand manuscript was
manufactured by a hoaxer (named Daniel Defoe, for instance),

certainly one's feeling toward the work would be very different, but the Pepys diary would not cease to be enjoyable. The same could hardly be said of Evelyn's. What gives ultimate meaning to the string of facts of more than a thousand months is that one man lived it all, sturdily and steadily himself through all the mutations of eighty-six years, only very rarely letting more than a day go by unrecorded, so that an entry such as the following is most uncommon: "There happen'd nothing this weeke worthy of note" (Jan. 4, 1685). On the contrary, he found noteworthy happenings, people, and ideas for year, after year, after year.

CHAPTER 6

Contributions to English Literature

IT is a century and a half since Evelyn's diary was first published; during this time, it has dominated his other works to such an extent that few but specialists or seventeenth-century scholars know much about the extent and variety of his literary career. There is no reason to suppose that the situation will alter greatly in the future. For literary merit, historical value, and human interest, the diary unquestionably is his most excellent work. But to establish general conclusions about Evelyn's distinctive qualities and relative importance, one must consider all of his literary compositions. Such a survey reveals the scope of his writings, something of his general literary intentions, his works of abiding interest, his contributions to the development of English literature, and the general style of his best works.

I *Scope and Aim*

The quantity of Evelyn's writings is immense. He kept his diary for almost eighty years. His letters number in the hundreds. He published eighteen books in his lifetime, and four more have appeared posthumously; several of the books are multiple-volumed affairs. He published three sets of incidental verses, two prefaces, and thirteen articles for periodicals and anthologies. His translations and editions of the works of others come close to a dozen. Editions and reprintings of his own works, issued under his supervision, total around forty. Many pieces still remain in manuscript, some of them interesting and complete enough to invite publication.

Evelyn wrote about almost everything under the sun, but gardening was his first and last love. Yet to say that scarcely hints at the multiplicity and mystery of that art, which encompassed, in Evelyn's writings, trees, shrubs, fruits, vines, and herbs, formal gardens, kitchen gardens, lawns, terraces, nurseries, and greenhouses, the daily duties and the annual round, the soil itself, the tools of the trade, and the manifold uses of all these trees, fruits, and vegetables. Then there were the other sciences, in the great seventeenth-century catch-all sense of the word "science." He did two medical essays; four on facets of geography; and treatises on city planning, air pollution, navigation, and commerce. He prepared directions for making bread, cider, wine, ink, relief maps and other models from wax, and a solution for rendering old manuscripts more readable. He wrote works on libraries, architecture, engraving, painting, and coins. History also attracted him: some of his science and art studies include historical surveys; two of his great incomplete projects are histories—of trades and of the Dutch War; and he completed histories of religion and of some national and local customs, compiled a saint's life and rogues' lives, and did much chronicle writing. He has pieces on politics, philosophy, and theology; half a dozen rules of life; and studies on French culture, child rearing, and idiosyncrasies of English manners and fashion.

This tremendous variety of subjects required a great range in literary genres. Essays, short and long, are the form Evelyn used most: factual exposition, political tracts, dedications, debates or rebuttals, literary criticism, historical pieces, essays of ideas, and meditations and prayers. More personal types of writing are the diary, his autobiographical sketch, rules of life, and letters. Among the more elaborate and formal genres, he wrote biography, character writing, courtesy literature, satiric prose and poetry, and complementary and other light verse.

Is Evelyn uncommonly diversified for his age? One way or another, the writings of Bacon, Browne, Robert Burton, and perhaps Locke and Bentley may touch on as many subjects as do Evelyn's, to say nothing of the range of such literary giants as Milton and Swift. However, these authors are so famous for one particular work or group of writings that their other subjects are overshadowed. Or they organized their works into some kind of system, as did Bacon. Scholars have tried to fit Evelyn's heterogeneity into one of his own large outlines, the *Elysium Britannicum* or the history of trades; but both of those projects exclude his personal, satiric, and religious writings—that is, several of his very best works. Is Evelyn an exception to his age, then, with no underlying plan or principal interest that accounts for both the bulk and the best of his work?

Quite the contrary, Evelyn had one aim, first and last throughout his work: the improvement of mankind. His abiding desire is social reform (in a broad pre-nineteenth-century sense) and the cultivation of every human faculty. He is very much the typical Renaissance encyclopedist, including all knowledge within his horizon. And it is the very vastness of his overall view that obscures its unity—the vastness and his by no means common emphasis on a social reform which is far too practical to be called speculative, yet far too immaterial to be called utilitarian. Sixteenth-century conduct books directed courtiers to take all knowledge, all refinements, every art and grace (temporal and spiritual) as their proper business. Evelyn followed this advice in his life and relayed it in his works.

If one calls his works an encyclopedia of courtesy literature, in the genuine humanist tradition, things fall into place. Every single work of his sets out to modify essentially the whole character of the reader—to enrich, purify, and strengthen his view of life. Gardening, trade, any particular pastime or phase of life is subordinate to this grand design. Spiritual and this-worldly, specialized and eclectic, Evelyn is always the layman speaking to laymen. More than that, he is always the man of ideals, pretending to no more virtue or ability than he had, but always putting his best side forward, always seeking to edify. Seen in this way, a great unity exists in Evelyn's work; and the multiplicity of his interests is entirely focused. Such a view illuminates Evelyn's career, establishes a relationship among his works, and provides some context for him in his period. It does not, however, measure him against his contemporaries in specifically literary terms.

II *Reputation and Influence*

Evelyn's position in English literature is clearly minor but also clearly enduring. His is a minor position because, among many other reasons, he never tried to achieve anything more. For one thing, many of his works make no pretense to art; they are surveys of facts or opinion, strictly unadorned expositions, with little or no literary relevance. Then, even in those works which did aspire to style and eloquence, at least half his mind was always on extraliterary results—like providing lumber for the navy, persuading fashion leaders to buy British styles, exposing impostors, or furnishing ethical and social principles and examples. Finally, but most central of all, he did not attempt any of the major literary genres: he wrote only light verse, never finished the one drama that he attempted, and wrote no fictitious narratives or romances. His literary aspirations were modest and thoroughly intermixed with utilitarian and functional goals.

But modest and minor do not necessarily mean insignificant. Evelyn made his mark and made it in two ways: he affected literary history, and he continues to be read. Evelyn's greatest impact upon literary history was made by his diary. One cannot prove that his faithfulness in keeping a diary encouraged others to do the same or that his example of content and style were directly influential, although the likelihood is great. But there is no dispute that the publication of his diary was the occasion for deciphering Pepys's diary, its publication and great popularity, and the subsequent publication of countless others. In these ultimate terms, the diary is then Evelyn's greatest contribution to English literary history.

But he made other contributions which were more immediate. Many of his subjects had previously received little or no literary attention and his treatment gave them prestige and currency. This statement is true for gardening, food, the arts, as well as for Lucretius and Epicureanism. Moreover, Evelyn was in the forefront of two fundamental changes in taste. He enjoyed landscape, both real and painted, long before it became the vogue; and his written expression of this enjoyment affected both literature and art. His decision to address his art studies to viewers, as well as artists, started a trend in literature. Also, he looked at nature with a new eye: he saw it realistically, rather than symbolically or conventionally; yet he esteemed it highly. The resultant literary treatment he gave to nature was without precedent, an early step in an important new direction.

He was a pioneer in some literary techniques. His was an early use of the device of the fictitious foreign traveler as satirist. He affected the course of courtesy literature, the Oriental tale, and biography; and he contributed to the increasingly polite tone of satiric verse. His defense of satire and his comments on the theory and method of translation are part of the growing body of literary criticism in these early days.

Even if Evelyn were never heard of again after 1706, his mark on the course of English literature would be significant. But for three centuries his works have been, and continue to be, read by new generations of readers. In the eighteenth century, the more technical works were the ones most often reprinted and prized as useful sources for practical information. Except for *Sculptura,* however, all his books became outdated or superseded for reference purposes after another hundred years. The response to Evelyn in the last hundred and fifty years alone counts in judging his lasting value.

The evidence is of three sorts. Many new editions and reprints continually appeared in the nineteenth century and are appearing even more frequently in this one.[1] Formal critical comment and reviews specifically on his work and the inclusion of him in littrary histories and surveys are an explicit indication of his reputation.[2] And there are casual references to him over the years in such literature as letters, journals, and familiar essays.[3]

The statistics on reprints together with the opinions of scholars agree that a dozen of his works continue to be read and commented on with pleasure. The diary and selections from the correspondence are, of course, pre-eminent. Next come *Sylva, Acetaria, Tyrannus, The Life of Mrs. Godolphin, Fumifugium, London Revived, The Character of England,* and *The History of Three Late Famous Impostors.* Three works published for the first time in this century—*A Devotionarie Book, Directions for the Gardiner,* and *Memoires for my Grand-son*—are too recently published for there to be an indication of how they will endure; but they were so favorably reviewed that they seem to share in the esteem accorded those that have been often reprinted.

II *Style: Conversational Structure*

Finally, there is the matter of Evelyn's style, about which critical statements are scarce. The few critics who have provided them tend to be brief and harsh. These men are among Evelyn's greatest admirers and have devoted years to editing and writing about his works. Still, they find much to lament in his style, make little effort to describe what is commendable, and even suggest that he wrote spontaneously and gave little thought to the question.[4]

But it cannot be chance that there is so close a resemblance between Evelyn's style and that of his contemporaries, most particularly Thomas Browne and Jeremy Taylor. Just about all the mid-century experimenters sought a written prose that approached the language as it is spoken and a simplified sentence structure, one close to the natural syntax of English. Different as their resultant styles are in other respects, their basic sentence patterns are alike: a series of loosely connected, short clauses, with the words in normal order. Their sentences are fairly long; but, since the thought is substantially complete early in the sentence, the length does not make for any real complexity.

Spontaneous as Evelyn's style looks, one must conclude that he deliberately fashioned it. He, too, was aware of the need for a more functional prose than English had ever had before; his letters and work with the Royal Society show this. Clearly this new, looser sentence structure represented for him the right approach because of its simplicity and flexibility. He adopted it uniformly from the start, adapted it to his own needs, and scarcely altered his style throughout his entire literary career.

The essence of Evelyn's style, accounting for both its effectiveness and its faults, is its conversational flavor. To the twentieth-century reader, this characteristic may not be overwhelmingly apparent. The frequently Latinate vocabulary, the prevalence of quotations from other writers (often in Greek, Latin, or Italian), and the length of the sentences (around seventy words on the average) are not characteristic of most people's speech, then or now, although it is imaginable that Evelyn spoke in some such whimsically erudite fashion. But the structure is very much that of spoken language, whether one looks at the sentences, the paragraphs, or the chapters. So is the presentation of ideas, in terms of their relationships. And so is the whole manner of address colloquial and loosely constructed.

Even in terms of overall structure, Evelyn's works are characteristically loosely organized. He always started with some kind of division of the subject, usually indicated in the list of chapters or in an introductory paragraph. But rarely is this division the best possible or even a very obviously logical one. The few exceptions are those in which he used a well-established literary convention or technique: *The State of France;* the preface to the translation of Chrysostom; *The Character of England; The Life of Mrs. Godolphin; The History of Three Late Famous Impostors.*

Here, he chose the form deliberately and exploited it with success and even with some originality. But, in the majority of his works, he digresses at will, sometimes for whole chapters, and he feels no need for rigorous selection or proportion. In the longer works, the reader's patience is tried, and sometimes the train of thought becomes quite lost. In the shorter pieces—*Fumifugium, Tyrannus, Directions for the Gardiner, Acetaria, Memoires for my Grand-son*—this casualness is close to being an asset, precisely because it produces an effect of spontaneity and artless sincerity.

Evelyn's sentences follow the natural order and construction of spoken English so that they sound as if they were coming right off the tip of his tongue, were being created even while the pen is moving across the paper. A sentence like this one from *Tyrannus* (1661) is typical: "Believe it, *La Mode de France* is one of the best returnes which they make, and feeds as many bellies as it clothes backs; or else we should not hear of such Armies, and Swarmes of them, as this one City alone maintains, who hang in the Ears, embrace the Necks and elegant Wasts of our fair Ladies, in the likeness of Pendants, Collers, Fans and Peticoats, with the rest of those pretty impediments, without which Heaven and Earth could not subsist."[5]

The first two words, "Believe it," establish the independent part of the sentence, and the explanation of what the reader is to believe is also completed promptly: the profitable nature of the fashion business. The proposal of an alternative, which follows, is very much a colloquial technique—forestalling objection before one is even voiced. This thought too is complete in itself, and a period could be placed after "maintains." "Who hang in the ears, embrace the necks and elegant wasts of our fair Ladies" does not identify or define or even describe the army of fashion designers in any restrictive sense. The clause starts as if it were a literal account of the way these parasitical designers hang on to their customers; then Evelyn suddenly switches the application by fancifully equating the couturiers with the costumes. There is no foreshadowing of this final development: the metaphor pops into the sentence in just the way that such a witty twist might be made in conversation.

An example from *Numismata* (1697) shows how little Evelyn's style changed in thirty years. Here again, the construction gives the effect of revealing how his mind was working. The sentence

starts with the phenomenon of the evil eye, a slight digression in
a series of anecdotes on the effects, both good and bad, of facial
expressions. This discussion of "aspect" is loosely tied in with the
topic of the chapter, physiognomy, which properly examines appearance only, not behavior. And Evelyn scarcely justifies the
presence of that subject in a book about coins. Yet one could
hardly want to dispense with this collection of recondite data:

No wonder then that some (perhaps innocent poor People) have
been accused for *Witches* and *Evil-lookers* as they call them; whiles
in the mean time, who can tell but that there may possibly be as
much danger in the Glances and Emissions of some *Bilious*, as of
Icterical Persons? or of such as Monsieur *Chauvin* (a *Parisian* Gentleman dwelling in *Diep*) who, the same Author affirms, he knew to have
so *Lyncean* and penetrating a sight, that using *Spectacles*, such acute
and keen Vapours darted from his Eyes, as in a short time, excavated
and wore out the very *Glasses* themselves, piercing the *Crystals* thro',
and rendering them useless, so as he was fain to be often supplying
them. (302)

As usual with Evelyn, the main clause is immediately set down:
the thought is that accusations of witchcraft are hardly surprising. At once, his lively imagination considers the contrary situation, the dangers of eyes which no one suspects. This possibility
brings to mind the anecdote about the lynx-eyed Frenchman,
which, in fact, has nothing to do with the evil eye except for its
fabulousness. The anticlimactic ending, the difficulty of keeping
such a man in spectacles, is rather characteristic of such a syntax
where many nonrestrictive elements succeed one another. The
effect is that of a loquacious speaker rambling a trifle aimlessly.

Evelyn's sentences often leave the reader yearning for more
pulling together, for a clarification of relationships, and for a better sense of emphasis. But perhaps it is not too specious to suggest, also, that much of the vitality of his writing derives precisely
from this random outpouring. The sketchiness of the presentation
stirs the imagination. And there is always the feeling that there
is no end to these strange and varied ideas that evolve in freely
associative fashion. The sentences can stop almost anywhere or
go on indefinitely, and so can the ideas.

IV *Style: Voice of the Narrator*

But what characterizes conversational style more strikingly than a certain syntax is the presence of a speaking voice, and Evelyn creates one in every one of his works. The personality of that voice differs from piece to piece. The fullness and richness and interest of the personalities vary, but always a definite voice is heard. The techniques that Evelyn uses to achieve this voice are the normal features of conversation: the use of the first person, the use of the second person and of imperative and hortatory forms, acknowledgment of the listener's personality, reference to his anticipated response, and expression of the speaker's position in relation to his topic. Even in the most subliterary, dryly expository of his writings, the audience is directly addressed and the "I" is usually identified in terms of his occasion for writing, the source of his material, and his degree of proficiency in this subject. In the more literary works, the identity becomes personal and affects the form and whole impact of the piece.

The deliberately fashioned "I" of *State of France* and *Character of England* is so marked by irony that one at once recognizes it as a fictive voice. Careful selection went into Evelyn's restrained self-characterization in *The Life of Mrs. Godolphin* and into the conventional voices of *Publick Employment . . .* and *A Devotionarie Book*. The likeness between the persona and Evelyn himself is far greater in *Tyrannus, Sylva,* and *Navigation and Commerce;* in fact, were it not for his own statements about each of these works, one might read them as pure Evelyn, so to speak.

But the effect of the speaker's voice is no less creative and genuinely literary in those works in which one can see no significant difference between the personality of the narrator and what one knows of Evelyn from the whole range of his writings. In fact, this may be Evelyn's most literary talent, not just in his diary but in all his works: the ability to make the voice of the narrator come alive with individuality, concern, and conviction. Eventually, this feature triumphs over every other element in his work. The facts that Evelyn arrays are fascinating, his tumultuous manner of presenting them is overwhelming; but, most of all, it is Evelyn's enthusiasm that confers upon this flood of material its special value for the reader.

When his books have been laid down and after the precise details have faded, much remains indelible: the seventeenth-century scene so clearly visualized with many of the people who appear in it and the esoteric bits of information and thought of the time. But far more important than any of these is that vividly characterized speaker volubly articulating his endless delight in this material. Whether Evelyn himself genuinely did enjoy life all that much is of no consequence. His works create such a point of view, embody, record, and indisputably communicate it.

Brilliant, stirringly exciting, profoundly dramatic occasions were neither frequent for Evelyn personally nor the preoccupation of his pen. If anything, he had a tendency to flatten waves rather than to stir them. But as one reads through his diary and other principal works, from early in one century to the beginning of the next, what emerges is a powerfully persuasive personality. There is little of pain, suffering, and human cruelty which does not appear somewhere in the pages of his works. But counterpointing these are quiet courage, undaunted faith, unswerving principle, a disciplined acceptance of life's monotony as well as its crises, a firm reliance on the stabilizing satisfactions of art and learning and employment. Many men have lived as long as Evelyn and as well. But not many have had the indefatigability, the enthusiasm, and the literary skill to capture and convey the experience with such detail and such conviction.

Notes and References

Chapter One

1. The passage in French reads: "Et c'est pourquoi le Diable est nommé Belial dans la Sainte Ecriture, comme qui diroit celui qui a voulu sécouer le joug, & ne dépendre plus de personne. Or puisque nous récherchons naturellement la liberté, & que nous fuions la servitude, non seulement comme le reste des animaux, mais encore davantage à cause de ce qui nous distingue d'eux, & de ce que nous avons de commun avec les Intelligences superieures, il s'ensuit que l'homme devroit être la plus libre de toutes les creatures d'ici bas. Si est-ce qu'il n'y en a point peut-être de plus esclave que lui en toutes façons." *Oeuvres,* nouvelle édition (Pfoerten, 1756), III, 192.

2. Ed. by William Derham, F.R.S. (London, 1726), pp. 186–88. The immediately subsequent article (pp. 188–90) is also by Evelyn, on the proper raw materials, mixture, and uses of ink for rolling presses; no account is given of the origin or occasion of composition.

3. George B. Parks, "John Evelyn and the Art of Travel," *Huntington Library Quarterly,* X (1947), 251–76. And see John Walter Stoye, *English Travellers Abroad 1604–67, Their Influence in English Society and Politics* (London, 1952), pp. 24–27.

4. W. G. Hiscock, *John Evelyn and His Family Circle* (London, 1955), p. 33. The letter is from Venice, April 20, 1647.

5. For the background on taste, see Henry V. S. and Margaret S. Ogden, *English Taste in Landscape in the Seventeenth Century* (Ann Arbor, 1955), pp. 37–38. I have retained the following passage all the vagaries of spelling; some are characteristic of Evelyn and the seventeenth century, but Evelyn wrote with disgust of the "innumerable Errata" in the work which, he alleged, "discouraged me with troubling the world with the rest" (Diary, May 12, 1656). The prefatory material which I quote is on unnumbered pages.

6. Wolfgang Bernard Fleischmann, noting that an evaluation of Evelyn's translation should properly consider which Latin text he used, supplies the available information before giving his own critique, *Lucretius and English Literature 1680–1740* (Paris, 1964), pp. 29–

33, 94. See also Thomas Mayo, *Epicurus in England* 1650–1725 (Dallas, 1934), pp. 43–51 and *passim*.

7. Letter to Taylor, April 27, 1656. The source in Gassendi is the Dedicatory Epistle of *De Vita, et Moribus Epicuri,* reprinted in *Opera Omnia* (Florence, 1727), V, 143. See Jeanne K. Welcher, "John Evelyn to Jeremy Taylor, 27 April 1656," *Notes and Queries,* NS XVI (October, 1969), 375.

8. W. G. Hiscock, "John Evelyn's library at Christ Church," *Times Literary Supplement* (April 6, 1951), p. 220

9. January 28, 1658, *Works of Sir Thomas Browne,* ed. by Geoffrey Keynes (London, 1931), VI, 301–2. Browne completed the essay *Of Garlands and Coronary or Garland Plants;* this is included in his complete works and was also printed separately in a limited edition for the Smith College Museum of Art (Northampton, Mass., 1962).

10. See Stephen Switzer, *Ichnographia Rustica* (London, 1718), pp. 58–60; James Dallaway's "The History of Modern Taste in Gardening," 1771, published as part of his edition of Horace Walpole's *Anecdotes of Painting* (London, 1826–28), IV, 288–89; George W. Johnson, *History of English Gardening* (London, 1829), pp. 103–8, 112, 136; Albert Sieveking, *The Praise of Gardens* (London, 1899), p. 370; Eleanour S. Rohde, *The Old English Gardening Books* (London, 1924), pp. 87 ff.

11. Max L. W. Laistner, *Christianity and Pagan Culture in the Late Roman Empire, together with an English Translation of John Chrysostom's Address on Vainglory and the Right Way for Parents to Bring Up Their Children* (Ithaca, 1951), pp. 77, 76 and 138, n. 29. Laistner notes that the French volume, taken directly from a manuscript, included both the Greek original and a Latin translation and that Evelyn availed himself of both versions (pp. 75–77).

12. Almost any section of the work illustrates the point; the quotations I give are from Laistner's translation, pp. 94–95 and Evelyn's, *Misc. Writ.,* pp. [113]–14.

13. (London, 1659). Besides early reprintings, *An Apologie* was issued in facsimile, introduction by Geoffrey Keynes, Augustan Reprint Society, Pub. No. 28 (Los Angeles, 1951), from which text I take my quotations. Keynes's introduction notes that Evelyn's diary reference to the publication of this pamphlet is wrong by several days.

14. *Newes from Brussels* is dated March 10, 1659 (presumably old style) and was published twice in 1660; the author is identified as Marchamont Needham. There was just the one edition of Evelyn's pamphlet in April, 1660. Both works are reprinted in *Misc. Writ.*

15. F. E. Budd, "A translation attributed to Evelyn: *The Manner of Ordering Fruit-Trees* (1660)," *Review of English Studies,* XIV (1938), 285–97. On the strength of Budd's arguments, Geoffrey

Keynes included *The Manner of Ordering Fruit-trees* when he revised *John Evelyn a Study in Bibliophily with a Bibliography of his Writings,* 2nd ed. (Oxford, 1968), p. 83.

Chapter Two

1. de Beer, III, 284, n. 4 *re* diary entry of April 24, 1661. A *Panegyric* is included in the facsimile edition of *An Apologie for the Royal Party,* cited above, from which text I take my quotations.

2. "Ballad of Gresham College," ed. by Dorothy Stimson, *Isis,* XVIII (1932), 115–16; see discussion in Marjorie Nicolson, *Pepys' Diary and the New Science* (Charlottesville, Virginia; 1965), pp. 148–49.

3. Review of *Memoirs, illustrative of the Life and Writings of John Evelyn, Quarterly Review,* XIX (April, 1818), 53.

4. As printed in Richard Baker, *Chronicle of the Kings of England,* ed. by E. Phillips (London, 1665), p. 799; the text of the original version is printed in Evelyn's *Memoirs,* 1st ed. (1818), II, 350–55.

5. The text from which I quote is that edited by William Bray, who labeled his "The Second Edition Enlarged" and incorporated the handwritten revisions from Evelyn's own copy of *Tyrannus.* Bray included this in Evelyn's *Memoirs,* 1st ed. (1818), II, 321–32.

6. See especially Walter Houghton, Jr., "The History of Trades: Its Relation to Seventeenth-Century Thought," *Journal of the History of Ideas,* II (1941), 33–60, and Grace Agnes Hawley, unpublished dissertation (Columbia, 1962), "John Evelyn and the Advancement of Learning."

7. *Catalogue of Engravers,* Vol. V, *Anecdotes of Painting,* ed. by James Dallaway, pp. 164–65.

8. The verses were for the second edition (London, 1664) and appear on unnumbered pages preceding the text; a new edition of the play, ed. by A. E. H. Swaen (Amsterdam, 1927), has a lengthy critical introduction.

9. "The Garden," first printed in Cowley's *Works* 1668, is included among the commendatory prefaces on unnumbered pages at the start of *Sylva* 1679.

10. "An Heroical Epistle of Hudibras to Sidrophel," 11. 47–48, appended to *Hudibras,* Part II, Canto III, ed. by A. R. Waller (Cambridge, 1905), p. 184; and see Butler, *Satires and Miscellaneous Poetry and Prose,* ed. by René Lamar (Cambridge, 1928), "The Elephant in the Moon in Long Verse," 11. 217–18, p. 22 and "Physique" (alluding to *Pomona*), p. 419. Evelyn is batted back and forth in a quarrel about the Royal Society, the quarrel taking the form of a series of pamphlets between Joseph Glanvill and Henry Stubbs,

1668–71; Grace Ann Hawley supplies a summary and bibliography, pp. 287–302 and nn.

11. Carson Duncan, *The New Science and English Literature in the Classical Period* (Menasha, Wisconsin, 1913), pp. 150–53. See also Edward Malins, *English Landscaping and Literature 1660–1840* (London, 1966), pp. 3 and *passim*.

12. See esp. Geoffrey Keynes, *John Evelyn, A Study in Bibliophily,* pp. 130–33, and Esmond de Beer, "John Evelyn, Fellow of the Royal Society (1620–1706)," *Royal Society of London Notes and Records,* XV (1960), 235.

13. *Sylva,* 4th ed. (1706), p. 62. It is this edition which I cite throughout this analysis of style.

14. *Ichnographia Rustica,* I, 58–59.

15. This quotation from the dedication to Charles II and the next, from the preface to Wren, come directly from the first edition, 1664; these prefatory pages are unnumbered. The only part of *A Parallel* reprinted in *Misc. Writ.* was "An Account of Architects and Architecture."

16. de Beer, introduction to the *Diary,* I, 18; Jane Lang, *Rebuilding St. Paul's After the Great Fire of London* (London, 1956), pp. 15, 158 ff.

Chapter Three

1. Issued first in 1665, this work was retitled *New Experiments and Observations Touching Cold or an Experimental History of Cold* (London, 1683). Boyle's remarks on Evelyn are on p. 160 of this 1683 ed.

2. Bray incorporated into his own commendation of Evelyn's "Snowpits" this passage from the *Biographia Britannia, Memoirs* (1818), I, xx.

3. Evelyn made revisions for later editions; my quotations are from that of 1675 in which the pages of the preface are unnumbered.

4. The bibliographic history is unclear but apparently the earliest extant complete text is "Evelyn's 'Discourse,'" *Royal Institute of British Architects Journal,* XXVII (1919–20), 467–70; it is from this source that I quote. In the same volume there are a series of papers on "London Town-Planning Schemes" (pp. 69–82) and an evaluation of Evelyn's discourse (p. 467).

5. *London Revived,* ed. by Esmond de Beer (Oxford, 1938), pp. 1–27.

6. In the prefaces, Evelyn vouched for but refused to name his sources. Scholars have since identified them; see Keynes, pp. 194–95; Michael Fixler, "A Note on John Evelyn's *History of the Three Late Famous Impostors,*" *The Library,* 5th ser. IX (1954), 267–68; and

Christopher Grose's introduction to his edition of John Evelyn, *The History of Sabatai Sevi, The Suppos'd Messiah of the Jews*, Augustan Reprint Society, Pub. No. 131 (Los Angeles, 1968).

7. Phyllis Greenacre, "The Impostor," *Psychoanalytic Quarterly*, XVII (1958), 359–82.

8. *A Devotionarie Book of John Evelyn of Wotton, 1620–1706*, ed. by Walter Frere (London, 1936).

9. George Rogers, *Oratio Anniversaria habita in Theatro Collegii Medicorum Londinensium, Decimo octavo die Octob. et divi Lucae Festo 1681* (London, 1682); Evelyn's verses are on p. 39.

10. *The Life of Mrs. Godolphin*, ed. by Samuel Wilberforce, Lord Bishop of Oxford, 1847. There were several new editions thereafter. The latest, based on the second mss., was by Harriet Sampson (London, 1939), from which I take my quotations.

11. See prefaces to the various editions; the unsigned review in *Gentleman's Magazine*, new ser. XXVIII (1847), 49–51; J. G. Lockhart's review in *Quarterly Review*, LXXXI (1847), 351–80; E. S. Roscoe, "A Seventeenth-century Friendship: John Evelyn and Margaret Godolphin," *Contemporary Review*, CXXXIX (1931), 78–84; and the *Times Literary Supplement* review of Harriet Sampson's edition, Dec. 9, 1939, p. 723.

12. *John Evelyn and Mrs. Godolphin* (London, 1951) and *John Evelyn and his Family Circle* (1955). Dissent from Hiscock's interpretations is found in reviews by *Times Literary Supplement* (Feb. 8, 1952, p. 106; James Holly Hanford, *Philological Quarterly*, XXXIII (1954), 272; Esmond de Beer, "John Evelyn: Mr. W. G. Hiscock's Account of Him," *Notes & Queries*, CCV (1960), 203–6; 243–48; 284–86; and Donald Stauffer, *English Biography Before 1700* (New York, 1964), Chap. 5.

13. Evelyn's verses—along with those of Aphra Behn, Nahum Tate, Thomas Otway, among others—were included in the second (1683) and subsequent editions of Creech's *T. Lucretius Carus his six books de Natura Rerum, Done Into English Verse*.

Chapter Four

1. *Directions for the Gardiner at Says-Court. But which may be of use for Other Gardens*, ed. by Geoffrey Keynes (London, 1932).

2. *History of Religion*, ed. by R. M. Evanson, two vols. (London, 1850).

3. *Memoires for my Grand-son*, ed. by Geoffrey Keynes (London, 1926), p. 64.

4. Charles Davies analyzes the poem, assuming Evelyn to be the sole author, "*The Rape of the Lock* and Evelyn's *Mundus Muliebris*—a Parallel," *Review of English Studies*, X (1934), 324–29.

Notes and References

5. *Athenae Oxoniensis: An Exact History of all the Writers and Bishops Who have had their Education in the University of Oxford, from 1500 to 1690,* 2nd ed. (London, 1721), II, 942–43.

6. To George Evelyn, Mar. 24, 1693, as quoted by Hiscock, *John Evelyn and His Family Circle,* p. 168; the letter is otherwise unpublished. See also Hiscock's " 'The compleat gardener,' " correspondence in the *Times Literary Supplement* (April 25, 1952), p. 281.

7. *Anecdotes of Painting,* ed. by James Dallaway, II, 78.

8. *Ibid.,* pp. 76–77, 79.

9. John Pinkerton, *Essay on Medals,* 3rd ed. (London, 1808), I, ix-x.

10. Royal Society of London *Philosophical Transactions,* III, no. 40 (Oct. 19, 1668), 799–801.

11. "An Account of divers Schemes of Arteries and Veins, Dissected from Adult Human Bodies, and given to the Repository of the Royal Society by John Evelyn," Royal Society of London *Philosophical Transactions,* XXIII, no. 280 (July and August 1702), 1177–1201.

12. Hiscock lists these manuscripts (pp. 243–44) and describes them *passim;* he summarizes and quotes from the unpublished letters (pp. 122–23), *John Evelyn and His Family Circle.*

13. See W. Lee Ustick, "Advice to a Son: A Type of Seventeenth-century Conduct Book," *Studies in Philology,* XXIX (1932), 409–41.

Chapter Five

1. The edition which I cite in the Preface above (H. B. Wheatley, ed., *Diary of John Evelyn,* 4 vols., London, 1906), while containing the largest number of Evelyn's letters of any of the printed collections, does not include all the published letters. W. G. Hiscock, a librarian at Christ Church, Oxford, where the Evelyn manuscripts are, used the unpublished letters copiously in his two books on Evelyn which I have cited several times above. Keynes refers to the manuscripts in his bibliography of John Evelyn. Francis Bowman started an edition of the letters some years ago, but it has been abandoned.

2. [James Hoste], "The Diarists of the Restoration," *The Quarterly Review,* CLXXXIII (1896), 2.

3. de Beer, "Introduction," *Diary,* I, 59–60.

4. The *Vita* is an incomplete recension of the diary made by Evelyn probably in the late 1690s, described by de Beer (I, 47 and 74) and included in the first volume of his edition of the *Diary;* the quoted passage is I, 54.

5. Almost every edition of Evelyn's diary, from the first appearance of the *Memoirs* (1818) onward, has had an introduction; most of these include critical evaluations. Quantities of reviews have greeted new editions, in both British and American periodicals. Comment has

appeared also in critical essays, studies specifically on Evelyn, and general studies. My generalizations are based on a survey of close to a hundred such criticisms, about a third of these prompted by the de Beer edition of 1955.

6. [Robert Southey], review of the *Memoirs, The Quarterly Review,* XIX (April 1818), 12.

7. W. Sichel, "Men who have kept a diary," *Blackwoods,* CLXV (1899), 73–74.

8. Introduction to *The Diary of John Evelyn,* ed. by Austin Dobson (London, 1906), I, lxix–lxx.

9. Introduction to *Diary of John Evelyn,* ed. by William Bray (Washington & London, [1901]), I, ix.

10. de Beer cites naval records and subsequent histories that indicate that Evelyn gave the wrong name for the yacht, as the "Mary" was lost in March 1675 (III, 80, n. 1).

11. "Rambling Round Evelyn," first published in 1920, reprinted in *The Common Reader,* 1st ser. (London, 1925), p. 120.

Chapter Six

1. See Geoffrey Keynes, *John Evelyn: A Study in Bibliophily.*

2. There is no complete secondary bibliography for Evelyn. See Jeanne K. Welcher, "A Survey of the Scholarship on John Evelyn," *Bulletin of the New York Public Library,* 73 (1969), 286–97.

3. No collection has been made of references to Evelyn found in these media, nor is there probably any great need in terms of the ideas expressed since the examples that come readily to hand show a uniformity of sentiment. Such diversified commentators as Wordsworth, Charles Lamb, Walter Scott, Henry Thoreau, Washington Irving, Benjamin Disraeli, C. S. Lewis assume that the name of Evelyn is a household word and that his comprehensiveness and careful detail are valued and enjoyed; there is often, too, a tinge of patronage, implying that Evelyn is too precise or proper.

4. Notably Ponsonby, pp. 238–44 and de Beer, "John Evelyn, F.R.S. (1620–1706)," *Notes and Records of the Royal Society of London,* XV (1960), 235–38. More sympathetic are Boas, *passim,* and Grace Hawley, pp. 152–53.

5. *Tyrannus,* in William Bray, ed., *Memoirs,* 1st ed., II, 324.

Selected Bibliography

PRIMARY SOURCES

1. *Collected Works*

The Miscellaneous Writings of John Evelyn. Ed., William Upcott. London: Henry Colburn, 1825. The only published collection of Evelyn's works contains almost all his books, many essays, the prefaces for most of the translations; Upcott's introduction, brief prefaces to individual works, and notes; and texts prompted by or replying to Evelyn's work. It omits the *Memoirs* and *Silva* (published separately as a set with this), *Numismata*, all the translations except the Chrysostom, and almost all the occasional pieces. A facsimile reprint of *The Miscellaneous Writings of John Evelyn*, 1825, is announced as a new subscription title in the series Anglistica & Americana, edited by Bernhard Fabian *et al.*, to be published by Georg Olms Verlag.

2. *The Diary and Correspondence*

Memoirs Illustrative of the Life and Writings of John Evelyn. Ed., William Bray. 2 vols. London: Henry Colburn, 1818. Selections from the diary and letters, with additions in subsequent editions.
The Diary of John Evelyn. Ed., William Bray, with a life of the author and a new preface by Henry B. Wheatley. 4 vols. London: Bickers & Son, 1906. The most complete selection of letters.
Diary of John Evelyn. Ed., Austin Dobson. 3 vols. London: Macmillan, 1906. Diary alone, with a useful critical introduction by Dobson.
The Diary of John Evelyn. Ed., E. S. de Beer. 6 vols. Oxford: Clarendon Press, 1955. Definitive edition with lengthy introduction, notes, and texts of the *Vita* and entire diary. Vol. VI is a very full index.
The Diary of John Evelyn. Ed., E. S. de Beer. Oxford Standard Authors. London: Oxford University Press, 1959. Single volume contains most of the diary (except sermon notes), part of *Vita*, very few notes, and full index.
John Evelyn's Diary. Ed., Philip Francis. London: The Folio Society,

1963. Consisting of 253 pages with ten illustrations, a pleasant introduction, and an index, this selection of highlights of the diary is the most appealing edition for the casual reader; its text is based on the de Beer edition.

3. Principal Single Works

Acetaria. A Discourse of Sallets. London: B. Tooke, 1699. *Misc. Writ.*, pp. 721–811. Reprint has brief critical foreword by Helen Fox. Brooklyn: Women's Auxiliary, Brooklyn Botanic Garden, 1937.

An Apologie for the Royal Party. N.p., 1659. *Misc. Writ.*, pp. 169–92. Facsimile reprint. Intro. by Geoffrey Keynes. Augustan Reprint Society, Pub. No. 28. Los Angeles: Clark Memorial Library, 1951.

A Character of England. London: J. Crooke, 1659. *Misc. Writ.*, pp. 141–67, based on the 3rd ed. (1659), containing the "Gallus Castratus" and Evelyn's reply, "A Letter in Vindication."

A Devotionarie Book of John Evelyn of Wotton, 1620–1706. Intro. by Walter Frere. London: Murray, 1936. First time published.

Directions for the Gardiner at Says-Court. Ed., Geoffrey Keynes. London: Nonesuch Press, 1932. First time published; has brief critical foreword.

An Essay on the First Book of T. Lucretius Carus de Rerum Natura. Interpreted and Made English Verse. London: Bedel & Collins, 1656.

Fumifugium: or the Inconveniencie of the Aer and Smoak of London Dissipated. London: Bedel & Collins, 1661. *Misc. Writ.*, pp. 205–42. Other editions have useful introductions: Ed., Samuel Pegge. London: B. White, 1772. Ed., Joan Evans. London: Swan Press, 1929. Same edition reissued, Old Ashmolean Reprints VIII. Oxford: R. T. Gunther, 1930. Ed., Rose Macaulay. Manchester, England: National Smoke Abatement Society, 1933. Ed., Arnold Marsh. London: National Society for Clean Air, 1961.

The Golden Book of St. John Chrysostom. London: Bedel & Collins, 1659. *Misc. Writ.*, pp. 103–40.

The History of Religion. Ed., R. M. Evanson. 2 vols. London: H. Colburn, 1850. First time published.

The History of the Three Late Famous Impostors. London: Herringman, 1669. Trans. into German 1669; altered version in French, 1683. *Misc. Writ.*, pp. 563–620. The Augustan Reprint Society, Pub. No. 131, reproduces the third section, "The History of Sabatai Sevi"; Christopher Grose's introduction gives historical context on Sevi and English attitudes toward the Jews. Los Angeles: Clark Memorial Library, 1968.

Instructions Concerning Erecting of a Library by Gabriel Naudeus.

London: Bedle, Collins, & Crook, 1661. John Cotton Dana's edition corrects typographical errors and supplies a brief introduction. Cambridge: Houghton, Mifflin & Co., 1903. *Advice on Establishing a Library* is largely a new translation of Naudeus' work, based in part on Evelyn's, as Archer Taylor explains in his introduction. Berkeley: University of California Press, 1950.

The Late News or Message from Bruxels Unmasked. London: Richard Lowndes, 1660. *Misc. Writ.,* pp. 193–204, with Marchamont Needham's *Newes from Brussels.*

The Life of Mrs. Godolphin. Ed., Samuel Wilberforce. London: William Pickering, 1847. First time published. Harriet Sampson used a second ms for her edition and supplied a critical introduction. London: Oxford University Press, 1939.

"Londinum Redivivum, or London Restored." The first full edition was *London Revived.* Ed., E. S. de Beer. Oxford: Clarendon Press, 1938.

Memoires for my Grand-son. Ed., Geoffrey Keynes. Oxford: Nonesuch Press, 1926. First time published; with a preface and notes.

Mundus Muliebris: or, The Ladies Dressing-Room Unlock'd. London: R. Bentley, 1690. Ascribed to Evelyn's daughter Mary, except for prefaces and "Fop-Dictionary" by him. *Misc. Writ.,* pp. 697–713.

"A Narrative of the Encounter between the French & Spanish Embassadours." In Richard Baker, *Chronicle of the Kings of England.* Ed., E. Phillips. London: Cotes, 1665, pp. 799–800. An earlier version was printed in the *Memoirs,* 1st ed. (1818), II, 349–55.

Navigation and Commerce. London: T. R., 1674. *Misc. Writ.,* pp. 625–86.

Numismata, A Discourse of Medals. London: Benj. Tooke, 1697.

Of Liberty and Servitude. Trans. from F. de la Mothe le Vayer. London: Meighen & Bedell, 1649. *Misc. Writ.,* pp. 1–38.

"Of Manuscripts." First printed in *Memoirs,* 1st ed. (1818), II, 334–48.

A Panegyric to Charles the Second. London: John Crooke, 1661. Reprinted with *An Apologie for the Royal Party.* Augustan Reprint Society, Pub. No. 28. Los Angeles: Clark Memorial Library, 1951.

Publick Employment and an Active Life Prefer'd to Solitude. London: Herringman, 1667. *Misc. Writ.,* pp. 501–52.

Sculptura: or the History, & Art of Chalcography & Engraving in Copper. London: Beedle & Collins, 1662. *Misc. Writ.,* pp. 243–336, with Evelyn's revisions (from 1755 ed.). A second part is included in an edition with critical introduction by C. F. Bell. Oxford: Clarendon Press, 1906.

The State of France. London: Bedel & Collins, 1652, *Misc. Writ.*, pp. 39–95.

Sylva, or a Discourse of Forest-Trees. London: Martyn & Allestry, 1664. The last edition made by Evelyn, 1706, included *Silva, Terra, Pomona, Acetaria,* and *Kalendarium Hortense.* Ed. with notes and life by A. Hunter. York: A. Ward, 1776. Ed. from 1706 edition with a lengthy critical introduction by John Nisbet. London: Doubleday, [1908].

"To Mr. Creech. On His Accurate Version of Lucretius." In Thomas Creech, *T. Lucretius Carus. The Epicurean Philosopher, His six books de Natura Rerum, Done Into English Verse.* 2nd ed. Oxford: Lichfield, 1683.

Tyrannus, or the Mode. London: Bedel, Collins, & Crook, 1661. Reprinted with Evelyn's corrections as 2nd ed. in *Memoirs,* 1st ed. (1818), II, 321–32. Facsimile of 1st ed. corrected in Evelyn's own hand, with critical introduction by J. L. Nevinson. Luttrell Reprints, No. 11. Oxford: Blackwell, 1951.

"Upon my Worthy Kinsman Colonel Tuke, His Incomparable Play." In Samuel Tuke, *The Adventures of Five Hours.* 2nd ed. London: Herringman, 1664. Ed with introduction by A. E. H. Swaen analyzing the commendatory verses as well as the play. Amsterdam: Swets & Zeitlinger, 1927.

SECONDARY SOURCES

BOAS, GUY. "John Evelyn, 'Virtuoso': In the Light of Recent Research," *"Essays by Divers Hands: Being the Transactions of the Royal Society of Literature,* NS XXVIII (1956), 106–22. Concise, graceful, critically sound account, with a few errors of fact.

CRAIG, E. GORDON. "John Evelyn and the Theater," *Mask,* X (1924), 97–115; 143–60. Reprinted in *Books and Theatres.* London: J. M. Dent & Sons, 1925.

DE BEER, ESMOND S. "John Evelyn, F.R.S. (1620–1706)," *Notes and Records of the Royal Society of London,* XV (1960), 231–38. Evelyn's activities in the Royal Society.

———. "King Charles II's Own Fashion: An Episode in Anglo-French Relations, 1666–1670," *Journal of the Warburg Institute,* II (1938), 105–15. The effect of *Tyrannus.*

DENNY, MARGARET. "The Early Program of the Royal Society and John Evelyn," *Modern Language Quarterly,* I (1940), 481–97. More detailed and lavish of praise than de Beer's on the same subject.

HAWLEY, GRACE AGNES. "John Evelyn and the Advancement of Learning," unpublished dissertation (Columbia, 1962). A comprehensive study of Evelyn's writings, leaning too hard on the thesis that the history of trades and Bacon's influence are the core of Evelyn's writings.

HILL, CHRISTOPHER. "The Diary of John Evelyn," *History*, NS XLII (1957), 12–18. Responsible, unusually critical review of the de Beer edition.

HISCOCK, W. G. *John Evelyn and His Family Circle*. London: Routledge & Kegan Paul, 1955. Most complete biography: uses material from unpublished mss.; little literary analysis; the same unproved inferences and lack of sympathy as in his *John Evelyn and Mrs. Godolphin* (1951)—see bibliog. of replies to that, *supra*, Chap. 3, n. 12.

————. "John Evelyn's Library at Christ Church," *Times Literary Supplement*, April 6, 1951, p. 220.

KEYNES, GEOFFREY. *John Evelyn: A Study in Bibliophily with a Bibliography of his Writings*. 2nd ed. Oxford: Clarendon Press, 1968. Primary bibliography fully annotated; fine collection of critical judgments.

KING, JAMES ROY. "John Evelyn and the new world of technology." *Studies in Six 17th-Century Writers*. Columbus, Ohio: Ohio University Press, 1965. Some insights together with some very strange judgments.

LASLETT, PETER. "The 'Scientist' in Seventeenth-Century England," *Cambridge Historical Journal*, XIII (1957), 183–86. Analysis of the term "scientist," showing Evelyn to be among the respectable amateurs of his day.

MARBURG, CLARA. *Mr. Pepys and Mr. Evelyn*. Philadelphia: University of Pennsylvania Press, 1935. Comparison of Pepys and Evelyn; seventeen previously unpublished letters.

O'MALLEY, C. D. "John Evelyn and Medicine," *Medical History*, XII (1968), 219–31. Demonstration of how unusually broad was Evelyn's acquaintance with medicine and medical men, as shown mainly by his writings.

PLUMB, JOHN HAROLD. *Men and Places*. London: Cresset Press, 1963. Very hostile essay on Evelyn.

PONSONBY, ARTHUR. *John Evelyn*. London: Heinemann, 1933. Biography, with good chapters on Evelyn's writings.

ROBBINS, CAROLINE. Review of Evelyn's diary, *Journal of Modern History*, XXVIII (1957), 392–93. Concise enumeration of the distinctive values of the diary.

SEYMOUR, WILLIAM. "John Evelyn and his Books," *History Today*, XVII (1967), 626–31. A brief account of Evelyn's writings, stressing his breadth of interests and learning.

TAYLOR, F. SHERWOOD. "The Chemical Studies of John Evelyn,"

Annals of Science, VIII (Dec. 31, 1952), 285–92. Survey and
evaluation of Evelyn's notes on chemistry, many in manuscript.
WILLEY, MARGARET. *English Diarists: Evelyn and Pepys. Writers and
Their Work,* No. 162. London: Longmans, Green & Co., 1963.
Very superficial short essay.
WOOLF, VIRGINIA. "Rambling round Evelyn." *Common Reader.* 1st
Series. London: Hogarth Press, 1925. Discusses the diary only.

Index

(The works of John Evelyn are listed under his name)

Index

Index